American Association:
A History

American Association of College and University Business Officers:

A History

Lanora F. Welzenbach

National Association of College and University Business Officers

Library of Congress Cataloging in Publication Data

Welzenbach, Lanora.
    American Association of College and University Business Officers.

    Bibliography: p.
    1. American Association of College and University Business Officers—
History. 2. Afro-American universities and colleges—United States—
Business management—History—20th century. 3. Segregation in
education—United States—History—20th century.
I. National Association of College and University Business Officers.
II. Title.
LB2341.95.U62A548   1985   378'.1'006.073   85-13891
ISBN 0-915164-26-4

Dedicated to
The Charter Members
Of the
Association of Business Officers in
Schools for Negroes
With Admiration and Gratitude
For Their Courage, Determination,
And Perseverance

Contents

Foreword

American Association of College and University Business Officers: A History is more than an account of the life of a professional organization. It is a record of the struggles and achievements of a dedicated group of men and women, the charter members and their successors, who persisted in bringing the best of professional knowledge and assistance to their jobs in the face of the social and economic strictures forced by segregation. Because of the efforts of many people of good will and the elimination of legally based segregation, the acute need for a separate association of black business officers ended in the early 1960s, and in 1967 the American Association was dissolved.

The American Association was a member of the National Federation of College and University Business Officers Associations, which existed from 1951-1962, and was represented from the beginning on the Federation's Board of Directors. Later, many members of the American Association also joined the National Association of College and University Business Officers (NACUBO) when that organization succeeded the National Federation in 1962. Several members of the American Association, including James W. Bryant, Burnett A. Little, and Harold K. Logan, served as officers of NACUBO.

It is with pride and pleasure, therefore, that NACUBO presents this history of the American Association, honoring with its publication the persons who worked so diligently from 1939-1967 to make that Association a superior organization for providing professional development to its member representatives and assisting in the improvement of financial administration of predominantly black colleges and universities. The story of the American Association offers an inspiring example to any professional group seeking to advance its field of endeavor.

Caspa L. Harris, Jr.
Past President, NACUBO

Preface

When the American Association of College and University Business Officers was dissolved in 1967, one of the stipulations mentioned in the Dissolution Resolution was that provision be made for writing a history of the organization. The next task was to find a person or persons with the time to undertake this work.

Originally, it was thought that someone who had been a member of the Association would prepare the history. But most of these people were still involved with professional activities, in their institutions or other positions, and in other association work, and no one felt sufficiently free to devote the necessary time and care required for such a project.

NACUBO's Minority Institutions Committee became interested in the history, realizing how important it was to document the activities of the American Association while many of its members were available to verify information and to enjoy the finished book. The committee therefore recommended to the NACUBO Board of Directors that the National Association undertake to produce a history of the American Association. The board approved, and in 1983 Caspa L. Harris, Jr., then president of NACUBO, appointed a Planning Committee, chaired by Luther H. Foster, Jr., to advise on preparation of the history. The Minority Institutions Committee, under the chairmanship of Robert D. Flanigan, Jr., maintained oversight responsibility for the project. (See the Acknowledgments section for lists of members of both the Minority Institutions Committee and the Planning Committee.)

Work on the history was assigned to NACUBO staff and completed in 1985. The task involved library research, the assistance of many people (see Acknowledgments), and a site visit to Tuskegee Institute, repository of the Association archives. This account does not claim to be the final word on the American Association, as more research on various aspects of the organization could be done. Indeed, it is hoped that this history may inspire other writers, such as doctoral students, to delve more deeply into areas that could only be discussed briefly here.

The book has six chapters, the first of which describes the historical background leading to formation of the American Association. The next five chapters present different periods in the life of the Association, including the first or formative years, World War II, the postwar period, the decade of the 1950s, and the decade of the 1960s until dissolution in 1967. In addition, nine appendixes document pertinent information concerning the Association, such as its purpose and its membership criteria, the officers and meeting sites for each year, and institutional members.

Publication of this history represents much more than the fulfillment of the stipulation drafted in the Dissolution Resolution of 1967. The book honors the dedication of men and women who worked for more than 28 years to bring the benefits of professional organization to business officers in predominantly black institutions. Many of those men and women went on to become member representatives of NACUBO, as well as of the regional associations, and to participate actively in the professional development of business officers through those groups.

In reading this history, it will be discovered that many of the issues facing college and university business officers do not change over the years. Accounting and budgeting, for example, have always been chief concerns of business officers and remain so at this writing. Also, an institution's physical plant and auxiliary services demanded much of a business officer's attention in the 1940s, as they do in the 1980s.

Other issues described in the history were special to particular periods, and changed with the circumstances. Such issues include greater government involvement in institutional affairs, fluctuations in student enrollment, and new attitudes concerning an institution's responsibility toward its students.

The major change recorded in this history is the revolution in social conscience that ended segregation and made it possible for members of the American Association to join fully the mainstream of professional life in their industry. If only for that reason, the story of the American Association has something of significance to say to everyone.

Robert D. Flanigan, Jr.
Chairman, Minority
Institutions Committee

Acknowledgments

Preparation of this history required the assistance of many people. First, the contribution of the Minority Institutions Committee is recognized, both for its oversight role in the project and for the review comments offered by committee members. Many thanks are due this committee for its interest and persistence in making possible the history's preparation and publication by NACUBO. (Members of the Minority Institutions Committee and of the Planning Committee for the History of the American Association are listed below.)

Special recognition is due the Planning Committee, whose members provided much resource material in the form of books, documents, and photographs. They were always available for extended consultations or to answer questions, and they went to extra effort to confirm information about which they were knowledgeable and to provide names of other valuable contacts.

Interviews with persons other than committee members produced information such as biographical and anecdotal material, a description of the World War II Pilot Training Program at Tuskegee Institute, and comments on the circumstances in which business officers at predominantly black colleges often found themselves. In this regard, particular recognition is given to Colonel (ret.) Herbert E. Carter and Margaret D. Welch of Tuskegee Institute, Alabama; Arthur Paul Davis of Washington, DC; and Milton Wilson of Howard University.

Preparation of the history required research in library collections and archives. In this connection, the librarians and assistants at the

Moorland-Spingarn Research Center at Howard University were very helpful. Special recognition is due to Daniel T. Williams, archivist at Tuskegee Institute, who facilitated the use of American Association archives by the author.

Following the list of committee members below are the names of other contributors and reviewers whose comments on relevant documents helped to establish some facts and aid in the interpretation of others. Each suggestion offered by reviewers was carefully considered in preparing the manuscript. In addition to their review, contributors supplied information about institutions, programs, and individual persons.

Finally, the efforts of David Jacobson, NACUBO editor, and Celeste Clair, publications assistant, helped to ensure that the final draft of the history would be stylistically smooth and well presented.

Perhaps the most important acknowledgment of all is to the early members of the American Association, whose day-to-day courage, determination, and dedication shine through the pages of Association Proceedings. The author is privileged to have been able to work with this admirable group of people, even at the distance of some years and often through the medium of the written word, rather than face to face.

Committee Members

Minority Institutions Committee

Robert D. Flanigan, Jr.
(*Chairperson*)
Spelman College

Sandra Altemeyer
Texas Southmost College

Maria Carlos
Saint Augustine Community College

Fred A. Gallot, Jr.
Alabama State University

Abraham Moore
Morgan State University

John V. Parham
Fayetteville State University

Planning Committee for History of American Association

Luther H. Foster, Jr.
(*Chairperson*)
Alexandria, VA

James B. Clarke
Washington, DC

Burnett A. Little
Baton Rouge, LA

Harold K. Logan
Tuskegee Institute, AL

Wendell G. Morgan
Washington, DC

A.L. Palmer
Howard University

Other Contributors and Reviewers

James W. Bryant
Rockledge, FL

Robert D. Carroll
Florida Agricultural and
  Mechanical University
Tallahassee, FL

Col. (ret.) Herbert E. Carter
Tuskegee Institute, AL

James B. Cephas
Colonial Heights, VA

Arthur Paul Davis
Washington, DC

Don A. Davis, Jr.
Newport News, VA

D.F. Finn
National Association of College
  and University Business
  Officers

Neal O. Hines
Seattle, WA

Sammye Jarmon
Texas Southern University
Houston, TX

Eugene Johnson
Hampton University
Hampton, VA

M. Maceo Nance, Jr.
South Carolina State College
Orangeburg, SC

G. Leon Netterville
Baton Rouge, LA

Abbott Wainwright
Washington, DC

Margaret D. Welch
Tuskegee Institute, AL

Daniel T. Williams
Tuskegee Institute
Tuskegee Institute, AL

Lucius Williams
Tuskegee Institute
Tuskegee Institute, AL

Milton Wilson
Howard University
Washington, DC

Lucius C. Wyatt
Hampton University
Hampton, VA

*Institutional Public Relations
  Offices*

Fisk University
Nashville, TN

Southern University
Baton Rouge, LA

Virginia State University
Petersburg, VA

1

Conditions Leading to Association

The American Association of College and University Business Officers (American Association) came into being in April 1939 as the Association of Business Officers in Schools for Negroes. Twenty-eight years later, in May 1967, the organization held its last meeting, at which it was formally dissolved and its members encouraged to seek membership in one of the regional associations of business officers.

Twenty-eight years is a brief life for such a group. Yet, the achievements of the American Association mark one of the more significant episodes in the history of American education and, when the time was right for its dissolution, the occasion was not one for regret (except for the understandable nostalgia any member feels for the loss of a well-loved and deeply respected organization); rather, it was a happy advance for the state of higher education in America.

The American Association, which was composed of predominantly black institutions, began with 25 charter members. At the time of its dissolution there were more than 60 members, and at least 82 institutions had held membership at some time during the Association's 28 years.

To understand the importance of the American Association to higher education and what it meant to its members, one must first consider both the early historical background and the more recent circumstances that prompted its formation.

Private Institutions for Blacks

The predominantly black institutions are concentrated in the South, where education for blacks was segregated from that of whites for most of the period from the end of the Civil War until the effects of the 1954 Supreme Court decision on desegregation (*Brown* v. *Board of Education*) began to be felt. In the decades preceding 1939— the year the American Association was formed—most institutions of education for blacks in the South were supported by church-related organizations rather than by public funds.[1] Many such schools had been established by missionary groups from the North, principally Baptist, Methodist, Presbyterian, and Congregational, with aid from the federally supported Freedmen's Bureau.[2] Many Northern white liberals, who were genuinely concerned over the economic fate of recently freed slaves, felt obligated to provide educational opportunities for the new citizens as a major step toward the integration of those citizens into American society.

With two or three exceptions, the mission schools and other private institutions (such as Hampton Institute, started in 1868 by General Samuel Chapman Armstrong, an agent of the Freedmen's Bureau)[3] began to be established shortly after the close of the Civil War. (Lincoln University in Pennsylvania, sponsored by the Presbyterian Church, and Wilberforce University in Ohio, sponsored by the Methodist Episcopal Church, had been founded respectively in 1854 and 1856.)[4] The efforts of most such schools were first directed to elementary and secondary education, since they were dealing with a largely illiterate population of ex-slaves. There was heavy emphasis on teaching trades and job-related tasks, in addition to some academic work, in order to prepare the new citizens for independent life. Gradually, higher education was added—although, in many cases, not until the early decades of the twentieth century[5]—and black students were trained in the professions, including medicine, law, and religion. However, both the generally low income of students and the hard facts of a segregated existence, with its limited job opportunities, meant that vocational training continued to be important.

Lag in Public Education

The growth of public educational institutions for blacks was much slower than that of black private institutions, in spite of legislation in the states providing for equal, although separate, education of the races. (The 1896 Supreme Court decision in *Plessy* v. *Ferguson* confirmed the validity of the "separate but equal" doctrine. The Court ruled in that case that Louisiana's requiring separate railway cars for "persons of color" did not violate the Constitution. This decision was not overthrown until 1954.)[6]

Poverty in the South

Reasons for the lag in public education for blacks stemmed partly from the general poverty throughout the South. As one chronicler points out:

> The low standards of education were particularly exaggerated in the Southern states where the economic chaos and poverty following the Civil War and Reconstruction period brought complications that could not easily be overcome. The Northern states had a taxable wealth far in excess of the Southern states, which meant that if the two areas were to have equal school funds, the South would have to pay taxes many times greater than the North.[7]

The situation was aggravated, of course, by the added expense of trying to maintain two separate school systems.

A further problem was that a basically feudal attitude toward education persisted in the South until well after the Civil War. As stated by Horace Mann Bond, president of Fort Valley State College, in the American Association's 1940 Proceedings:

> Higher education was the birthright of the "gentleman." The University was not for the poor white boys. . . . If a poor white boy would have been an outcast at the University of Alabama in 1860, you can imagine the accumulated attitudes with which higher education for Negro ex-slaves was greeted in 1865 and in the generation following.[8]

Whatever the reasons, a sharp disparity existed in the amount of state funds appropriated for white and black institutions. Papers presented at various meetings of the American Association indicated that this disparity was a continuing problem faced from the beginning by business officers of black institutions. One example is shown in Dallas C. Brown's 1941 address, "The Financial History of Black Higher Education in West Virginia," in which he pointed out that in 1939 West Virginia State College (black) received $220,716 in support, while $1,267,001 was spent on West Virginia University (white). That year the state college had about 1,000 students while the state university had approximately 3,000 students. Judging by this ratio, for the educational support to have been equal, the state college for black students should have received twice the amount it was given, or $442,333.[9]

A thoughtful paper presented by Doxey A. Wilkerson, associate professor of education, Howard University, at the first, or organizational, meeting of the American Association discussed "The Allocation of Public Funds for Higher Education among Negroes." Dealing principally with land-grant colleges, the paper noted federal legislation that guaranteed an equitable distribution of federal funds to these colleges:

> The original provision in the Second Morrill Act, continued in its two sequels, requires that "no money shall be paid" to any state with separate white and Negro land-grant institutions unless the legislature of such state shall "propose and report to the Secretary of the Interior a just and equitable division of the fund . . . between one college for white students and one institution for colored students . . . which [fund] shall be divided into two parts, and paid accordingly."[10]

Nevertheless, this stipulation was largely ignored and inequities prevailed. To quote from the same paper:

> It is apparent from [certain] analyses that the Negro land-grant colleges of the South are forced to operate on a plane of financial support which is markedly below that of the corresponding white institutions in the same states.[11]

Tables and statistics given in the paper support this allegation, and afford some idea of the handicap that hampered the work of business officers from black colleges.

Growth of High Schools for Blacks

Throughout the South, publicly supported high schools for blacks were also slow in coming. The general poverty of the area has been mentioned, and an unenlightened, often hostile white majority was scarcely willing to be taxed for black elementary schools, let alone for secondary institutions. Virginius D. Johnston, then treasurer of Howard University, stated in an address to the third meeting of the American Association in 1941 that in 1913 there was only one four-year accredited high school for blacks in the entire state of Virginia.

He added that he considered this situation to be typical of those states with a separate system of education for blacks. Johnston went on to say that in the school year 1930-31, the number of accredited four-year high schools for Virginia's black students had increased to 23; in 1938-39, the year that the American Association was formed, the number had risen to 60. This growth was also evident in other Southern states.

Rising enrollment posed problems for business officers at black institutions, for it substantially increased the burden on these institutions to find funding to educate the additional students prepared for them by the secondary system.[12] Figures taken from the 1940 Proceedings indicated that in 1916 there were 2,637 persons listed as students in black colleges; in 1938 the number had risen to 35,000.[13] This increase probably was partly due to the meagerness of job opportunities for young black people and partly to their growing awareness of developing educational opportunities. The United States was still struggling out of the Great Depression and the economic situation was bleak. With jobs so scarce, more young blacks were entering the colleges—where, incidentally, work was available to help them through.

Administration of Small Institutions

The administration of institutions of higher education, particularly of the small private colleges, both black and white, was considerably less complex in the late nineteenth century and early twentieth century than in the 1970s and 1980s. It can be said that in many cases the college president (who often was white, even in the case of black colleges) and the governing board managed all aspects of administration, from academic affairs to the business function. Often, a casual approach to financial administration in those early years presented an additional obstacle to the progress of small, struggling colleges.

It should also be noted that certain black colleges of that time had excellent business and financial administration, guided by such astute, forward-looking men as V.D. Johnston, mentioned above; Luther H. Foster, Sr., of Virginia State College for Negroes; Don A. Davis, of Hampton Institute; and J.R.E. Lee, Jr., of the Florida Agricultural and Mechanical College for Negroes. These four were particularly instrumental in activities designed to further good business practice and, eventually, in providing a frame of reference for those activities by founding the Association of Business Officers in Schools for Negroes.

Foster and the General Education Board

The excellent business and accounting management that Luther Foster, Sr., exercised at Virginia State brought him to the attention of the General Education Board, which was founded by John D. Rockefeller, Sr., in 1902. The board, which became a major contributor to black education in the South, had its genesis in the interests of a Northern businessman, Robert D. Ogden, who was deeply concerned with education in the United States and who organized a trip by special hired train in 1901 to visit some outstanding black schools. Among the guests on the journey was John D. Rockefeller, Jr., who was influenced by that experience to approach his father with an idea for assisting in the improvement of education in the South. The General Education Board, whose announced purpose was "the promotion of education within the United States without distinction of race, sex or creed," was the result.[14] Before it made the last of its major grants in the 1960s, the board's many activities included aid for rural schools, high schools, medical schools, farm demonstration programs, and college administration.

Of greatest significance to the present history was the General Education Board's assistance in improving the financial and business practices of colleges and universities. This assistance came about through the board's concern that, should it give money to these institutions, it was "essential that recipient institutions be acquainted with sound financial practices before handling it."[15]

Investigation by the board revealed that often there was no bookkeeping staff of any kind at a given college. Many college presidents were former clergymen with no training in or understanding of business procedures. "One college," according to an account by Raymond B. Fosdick of the General Education Board, "was discovered which had no record of bonds given for endowment except the envelope in which they were placed."[16] Stories were told of small institutions— whether for white or black students—at which college presidents kept college records in a desk drawer, or simply stored them in their heads.

The association of Luther Foster, Sr., with the General Education Board was fruitful for both the board and the black institutions Foster wished to help. In the 1941 Proceedings of the American Association, Foster described a study, performed by him under the auspices of the board about 18 years previously, of the 17 black land-grant colleges in the South. Assisting him in his study had been W.J. Hale, president of Tennessee State College, and Charles E. Mitchell, business manager of West Virginia State College. Foster quoted part of a report on the conditions discovered by the three men. The report had been written, according to the quotation, with the intent "to reveal bases for improvement, and with this in mind it . . . selected . . . facts as representative of general conditions and of some of the points which the various presidents will probably desire to improve."[17] He continued with a detailed account of problems encountered at the various schools, including dilapidated physical plants, irregular and inefficient purchasing, lack of proper budgets, difficulties in feeding and housing students, and other ills. At the end of his address, however, Foster stated that he was happy to be able to say that in the "financial affairs of these schools today [1941] much progress has been made in business operations."[18]

A man who worked closely with Foster, Sr., and his colleagues was the University of Chicago's Trevor Arnett, whose 1922 publication, *College and University Finance*, was a basic contribution to college fiscal management. Arnett became secretary of the General Education Board in 1920 and its president in 1928. Arnett's admiration for Foster's financial "wizardry" at Virginia State led him to seek the latter's assistance in determining the merit of requests for board funds made by other black institutions. From 1929 until his death in 1949, Foster acted as financial advisor to black colleges receiving funds from the board. This service involved visits to many other colleges and evaluations of their programs. Foster also worked with the Julius Rosenwald Fund, a foundation of the time that made some modest grants to certain black institutions.[19]

Need for Better-Trained Managers

Foster realized that improving the management at colleges everywhere depended greatly on having better-trained business officers. Institutional presidents and boards had to be persuaded that they needed responsible, knowledgeable fiscal managers on their staff— not, as was often the case, a treasurer who lived in a city apart from the institution and rarely had contact with its day-to-day operations. With funds from the General Education Board, Foster launched an internship program at Virginia State, in which promising graduates from black colleges were given an opportunity to work in all phases of business management at the college.[20] A number of young men who interned in this way went on to take responsible positions in other institutions.

James B. Clarke, who eventually became treasurer of Howard Uni-

versity, went from Foster's intern program to the State College for
Colored Students, in Dover, Delaware. "I wasn't really very interested in taking a job in Delaware," Clarke said, smiling as he remembered the experience. But Foster was persuasive and knew how
to push his selected interns in the right direction. Aware that the
State College at Dover did not have a regular staff business manager,
Foster insisted that "they really need somebody up there," until
Clarke gave in and took the job, which started him on a long and
successful career in college business administration.[21]

Such internship programs were invaluable in demonstrating what
a well-trained business officer could do for an institution, but it
became increasingly evident that a more broad-based means of assistance, available to a larger number of persons, was necessary. The
one-to-one training offered by an apprenticeship program was not
sufficient to meet the needs of institutions that were growing in size
and complexity.

Problems Posed by Segregation

The opportunities for professional improvement afforded by formal associations of business officers seemed to Johnston, Foster,
Don Davis, and others to offer such assistance. Both Johnston and
Foster had attended meetings of the Eastern and Central Associations
of College and University Business Officers (EACUBO and CA-
CUBO) and had been impressed with the benefits of exchanging ideas
in a gathering of fellow managers, as well as with the knowledge
and suggestions that could be gained from listening to speakers who
were experts in areas of great concern to college administrators.

However, there was a major stumbling block for predominantly
black institutions that were seeking association. The great majority
of such colleges were in the South, and SACUBO, the Southern
Association of College and University Business Officers, did not
accept black administrators. Johnston and Luther Foster, Sr., who
were very light in color, and Robert O. Purves, who was white and
was then at Hampton Institute, had been able to attend meetings of
the Eastern Association. Still, even the Eastern Association was cool
at first to the notion of having blacks among its members. Howard
University applied for membership in EACUBO in 1942. This resulted in a policy decision that additional members of the American
Association, other than Howard, would not be admitted. So much
protest greeted this decision—including strong reactions from college presidents—that the policy was clarified, allowing admission

of all institutions eligible for membership in the Association of American Colleges, an organization that included very few of the black colleges. It was on that basis that Howard became a member of EACUBO. Finally, in 1960, EACUBO's membership criteria were changed, allowing any institution granting a baccalaureate degree or higher to be admitted.[22] (Two-year colleges are also admitted to EACUBO at this writing.) Admission to CACUBO was not a problem, but very few predominantly black colleges were located in that region.

In closing its doors to blacks, the Southern Association followed a policy in use by most organizations in the 1920s and 1930s. Professional job opportunities almost did not exist for blacks. An article in the August 1938 issue of *In Crisis*, the magazine published by the National Association for the Advancement of Colored People (NAACP), illustrated the dilemma of black college graduates, in this case from a white institution in the North:

> When the employing interviewers come to the campus from Standard Oil, Western Electric, General Electric, United Fruit Company, the big finance companies and the nation's premier department stores, the farthest thing from their minds is a Negro filling any of the positions in their organizations.[23]

Foster's son, Luther H., Jr., who had a master's degree in business administration from Harvard University, was told not to bother to apply for a job with any established accounting firms. Blacks who did accounting work could not join community professional associations. Their job opportunities were limited almost entirely to teaching or administrative work in black institutions. (Job opportunities remained scarce for blacks into the 1950s, a circumstance that underscores the importance of the American Association's placement service—see pp. 28 and 73.)

Thrust Toward Association

The segregation policies that kept bright, young black professionals out of so many areas worked to the advantage of the institutions in at least one respect: black institutions did not need to fear a "brain drain" to the much more affluent white sector. With the best of their students forced to seek employment within a limited sphere, black institutions were almost guaranteed the chance to hire the best of black talent. Further, since black business officers were denied

so many opportunities for fellowship with white colleagues, they
came to form a very close communion among themselves, an in-
terdependence and mutual support system that helped them through
many difficult situations. Nevertheless, coming up against so many
blank walls was, at the least, discouraging.

The story is told of a Christian missionary who, when confronted
with the overwhelming misery and ignorance of a backward area, is
said to have stated that "it is better to light a candle than curse the
darkness." This declaration of determined optimism could have been
the motto of Foster, Johnston, Davis, and others when they set out
to form the Association of Business Officers in Schools for Negroes:
this organization was the lamp that would brighten the way for black
college business officers for almost 30 years, until the rising con-
sciousness of blacks and a developing conscience among whites would
finally create conditions making the Association no longer necessary.

References—Chapter 1

1. Doxey A. Wilkerson, Howard University, "Allocation of Public Funds
   for Higher Education among Negroes," 1939 Proceedings of the
   Association of Business Officers in Schools for Negroes.
2. Dallas C. Brown, West Virginia State College, "The Financial History
   of Higher Education for Negroes in West Virginia," 1941 Proceedings.
   Horace Mann Bond, Fort Valley State College, "The Support of Public
   Higher Education in Alabama, 1865-1930," 1940 Proceedings.
   A.S. Parks, Florida A&M College, "The Financial History of Higher
   Education for Negroes in Florida," 1948 Proceedings.
   Raymond B. Fosdick, *Adventure in Giving: The Story of the General
   Education Board* (New York and Evanston: Harper & Row, 1962).
3. Robert O. Purves, Hampton Institute, "Student Labor As Applied to
   Construction Work at Hampton Institute," 1939 Proceedings.
4. Alan Pifer, "The Higher Education of Blacks in America," address
   delivered under the auspices of the South African Institute of Race
   Relations, Johannesburg, 1973, pp. 13-14.
   William Hannibal Robinson, *History of Hampton Institute, 1868-
   1949* (New York: New York University, 1953).
5. Parks, "Financial History," 1948 Proceedings.
6. Pifer, *The Higher Education of Blacks in America.*
7. Fosdick, *Adventure in Giving*, p. 2.
8. Bond, "Support of Public Higher Education," 1940 Proceedings, p. 34.

9. Brown, "Financial History," 1941 Proceedings.

10. Wilkerson, "Allocation of Public Funds," 1939 Proceedings, p. 104.

11. Ibid., p. 108.

12. V.D. Johnston, Howard University, "Some Problems Immediately Ahead of the Business Officer," 1941 Proceedings.

13. F.D. Patterson, Tuskegee Institute, "Cooperation and Integration of Objectives of Higher Education among Negroes," 1940 Proceedings.

14. Fosdick, *Adventure in Giving*, p. 8.

15. Ibid., p. 137.

16. Ibid., p. 138.

17. Luther H. Foster, Sr., Virginia State College, "Some Gains in the Financial Procedures and Practices in Negro Colleges," 1941 Proceedings, p. 23.

18. Ibid., p. 25.

19. Rayford W. Logan and Michael R. Winston, *The Dictionary of American Negro Biography* (New York: W.W. Norton, 1982), pp. 239-240.

20. Ibid.

21. James B. Clarke, interview with author.

22. Emily H. Webster, *Eastern Association of College and University Business Officers: Fifty Years in Review, 1919-1969* (EACUBO, 1969).

23. G. James Fleming, "After Jimmy Graduates, What?" *In Crisis*, v. 45, no. 8 (August 1938), p. 264.

2

Organization and Early Years: 1939-1941

No records could be found that document the conversations, telephone calls, or correspondence that must have preceded the first meeting of a proposed new organization of business officers in schools for Negroes. Discussion of such an association may have begun several years before definitive plans were made to call business officers together for the purpose of organizing such a group. Or action may have followed swiftly after an initial decision on the part of a core group of business officers that such an organization was necessary. According to Margaret D. Welch, who served as secretary to Virginius D. Johnston at Howard University for 17 years, files concerning the beginning of the American Association existed at one time at that university.[1]

Founders of the Association

Whatever the particulars of the American Association's origins, four names are referred to in the Proceedings of the early years as being pivotal: V.D. Johnston; Luther H. Foster, Sr.; Don A. Davis; and J.R.E. Lee, Jr. These men, who were instrumental in forming the Association for Business Officers in Schools for Negroes, as it was first called, shared a background of hard work, community service, and intellectual achievement and brought a broad range of individual talents to the new organization.

Virginius D. Johnston

Virginius Douglas Johnston, who was treasurer at Howard University when the American Association came into being, was born in Petersburg, Virginia. He was a graduate of Northwestern University in Evanston, Illinois, in which city he worked in insurance, both during the time he attended the university and after graduation. Eventually he went to Howard University as its budget officer (he had been employed there "several years" before Mrs. Welch, then Margaret Davis, came to work as his secretary in 1932).

Mrs. Welch indicated that Johnston, of the four or five men most interested in association, was the one who actually made the move to set up a formal organization. This appears to be borne out by a resolution offered at the 1949 American Association meeting, on the occasion of Johnston's leaving higher education for private industry. Johnston, known by his colleagues for his modest, quiet demeanor, fought the evils of segregation throughout his life.

"He wrote the first letter to *The Washington Post* that protested Marian Anderson's 1939 debarment from Constitution Hall," Mrs. Welch stated in an interview. Largely through a letter-writing campaign initiated by Johnston on behalf of Miss Anderson, the great singer was later asked to perform at the Lincoln Memorial.

Johnston was greatly concerned with the professional development of business officers. Since he had found so much of value in attending meetings of EACUBO, he attempted to bring several of the people on his staff at Howard University to one such meeting. When he inquired about the feasibility of this move, explaining that his colleagues were Negroes, he was told that he could bring them if they were light-skinned, like himself.

"He was furious," Mrs. Welch recalled. "He began to write to presidents of institutions that had business officers in EACUBO, to protest the segregation. And I think that may have been what made him decide that there really had to be an association for black business officers."[2]

Luther H. Foster, Sr.

The financial acumen and organizational ability of Luther H. Foster, Sr., was indicated in Chapter 1 in connection with his work both at Virginia State College and with the General Education Board. Foster was born in 1888 and gained his first experience of the world of business by engaging in part-time farm work and clerking in his father's general store. He was graduated from St. Paul's Institute in

Lawrenceville, Virginia, and taught one year in the public schools before returning to St. Paul's to serve a three-year apprenticeship in the Institute's business office. He was employed by the Institute as head bookkeeper from 1911 to 1913, when he went to Virginia State College. There he served as treasurer and business manager until 1943, as acting president for a year, and finally as president of the college until his death in 1949.[3]

Don A. Davis

Don A. Davis, of Hampton Institute, was another important force behind the organization of black business officers. Davis's brother, Arthur Paul Davis, of Washington, DC, stated that Davis was the third of eight children. Their father had been born into slavery. Don Davis graduated from Hampton Institute, which was then a secondary school, and in addition took several correspondence courses. Eventually he was to see two of his children graduated from Dartmouth College.

According to A.L. Palmer, assistant to the vice president for health affairs, Howard University, and a former president of the American Association, Davis was known among his colleagues as the "dean of business officers." This title paid tribute both to his longevity in office and to his expert training of the many persons who worked for him and later went on to become chief business officers. "Don was well-liked," his brother observed, "and popular with all who knew him."[4]

In 1954 Davis was awarded an honorary master of arts degree from Hampton Institute, then a full degree-granting institution. He worked in Hampton's business office in many capacities, beginning as a clerk in 1910 and retiring in 1957 as the Institute's business manager.[5]

J.R.E. Lee, Jr.

J.R.E. Lee, Jr., is the fourth name that stands out among those who organized the American Association. His interest in working in higher education was encouraged by his father, who taught in several black colleges and eventually became president of Florida A&M University. Lee, Jr., began his employment at Florida A&M in 1924 and was business manager there in 1939, when the American Association was formed. Later, in 1957, he was named vice president.

Lee was graduated from Lincoln University in Pennsylvania and began his working career as a salesman with the Adams Department Store, Muskogee, Ohio. Before accepting a position at Florida A&M,

Lee, Jr., assisted his father in organizing a project that was to become the National Business League, which existed to serve the business interests of Negroes. This experience gave Lee a "unique opportunity to . . . make first-hand appraisals of the civic, professional and economic status of his people in every section of this country"[6] and also helped prepare him for his administrative work at the university and for his part in founding the American Association.

First Meeting

Howard University, Washington, DC, hosted the first, or organizational, meeting of the new association on April 13-15, 1939. Segregation policies meant that participants could not meet in one of the community's hotels where their white colleagues would have had such a gathering, so it fell to the various member colleges to provide both meeting rooms and sleeping accommodations.

The meeting took place in the newly opened Founders Library. Howard University had been established by an Act of Congress in 1867, when a charter for the institution was approved to develop the following departments: normal, collegiate, theological, law, medical, agriculture, and "any others desired." General Oliver Otis Howard, a white man who was a West Point graduate and first commissioner of the Bureau of Refugees, Freedmen, and Abandoned Lands (i.e., the Freedmen's Bureau, established in 1865), was largely responsible for the passage of the bill that created the university. From 1869 to 1874, Gen. Howard was the third president of the institution, which bears his name.[7]

Howard University came into being partly as an attempt to educate the newly freed blacks who streamed into the District of Columbia following the Civil War (in 1860 there were approximately 10,000 black people in the District; by 1866 the number had grown to 43,000). It was Gen. Howard's intention that the institution should be open to everyone who desired to study, without regard to race, sex, or creed, but an increasing drive toward segregation meant that Howard University became, in practice at least, a predominantly black institution.[8] That was the situation when its treasurer, Virginius D. Johnston, offered the campus as the meeting site for the first gathering of the American Association.

Response to the call for organization was heartening. Approximately 117 black institutions, public and private, existed in 1939,[9] and that first year saw 39 become members (see Appendix 2 for a list of charter members). Twenty-five schools sent a total of 38 representatives to the first meeting, each institution sending from one to eight persons. Such attendance indicated a significant interest in the new association, since the meeting involved a certain cost and the economy of the country as a whole and of the South in particular had not yet recovered from the Great Depression.

Congratulatory letters and telegrams greeted the beginning of the American Association. The occasion offered a notably substantive program—a characteristic that was to become a hallmark of American Association meetings. Featured speakers included nationally known figures, such as J. Harvey Cain of the Financial Advisory Service and Jackson Davis of the General Education Board, and knowledgeable business practitioners from various member institutions.

At that first meeting the American Association adopted an unwritten policy of inviting the president of a member institution to each annual gathering. The purpose of such invitations was to allay concerns that might be generated over the possibility of business administrators venturing into areas of presidential prerogative. John W. Davis, who attended the 1939 meeting and was president of West Virginia State College, was a trusted advisor and counselor both to the Association and to the presidents concerned.[10]

Luther H. Foster, Sr., presided at the opening session. The first order of business was the appointment of a Committee on Organization, which was charged with the responsibility of working out the details for permanent organization. The chairman of this committee was J.R.E. Lee, Jr., Florida A&M College. Other members were Lloyd Isaacs, Tuskegee Institute; J.H. Carter, Morgan College; Charles R. Rutherford, West Virginia State College; and V.D. Johnston, Howard University.

In the absence of a nominating committee, the Committee on Organization took the responsibility for nominating the first officers of the new association, who were as follows:

> President: Luther H. Foster, Sr.
> Vice President: J.R.E Lee, Jr.
> Secretary: V.D. Johnston
> Treasurer: Charles R. Rutherford

The committee also nominated three other persons to complete an Executive Committee: Edmund H. Burke, Tuskegee Institute; Robert O. Purves, Hampton Institute; and Harold K. Logan, Wiley College.

Recommendations for Organization

The Committee on Organization made seven recommendations, which are quoted below from the minutes of the 1939 meeting:

Report and Recommendations of the Committee on Organization

Your Committee on Organization of the Association of Business Officers in Schools for Negroes offers for your consideration the following report and recommendations:

(1) *Organization*: We recommend the establishment of a permanent organization of Business Officers in Schools for Negroes. It is further recommended that this organization be known as the Association of Business Officers in Schools for Negroes.

(2) *Membership*: All educational institutions, with a rating of Junior College or higher, will be eligible for membership in the association of Business Officers. All institutions represented at this meeting will become charter members of the Association if they desire.

(3) *Meetings*: It is recommended that the Association hold one meeting each year at a place selected by the Institution that has been designated by the Association as host of the annual meeting. The host Institution for each successive meeting will be named by the Association at its annual meeting. The date of each annual meeting will be decided by the Executive Committee and said Committee will advise or have the Secretary of the Association advise each member of the date selected at least ninety days prior to the meeting.

(4) *Officers*: It is recommended that at each annual meeting the following officers be elected to serve for a period of one year or until their successors are elected:

President, Vice-President, Secretary, Treasurer.

It is desirable to try as far as possible to consider the different sections of the country in the election of officers.

(5) *Committees*: An Executive Committee of seven members will act for the Association when it is not in session. The Executive Committee will be composed of the four

officers and three other members to be elected by the
Association at each annual meeting. Any other temporary
or permanent committees may be appointed or elected as
the need arises.

(6) *Fees*: It is recommended that the annual fee for all
member institutions be $10.00 per year, due and payable
not later than the 15th of May of each year. The first such
payment is to be made not later than May 15, 1939.

(7) *Objectives*: The objectives of the Association will be
drafted by the Executive Committee and circulated among
members of the Association prior to the next annual meeting. It is suggested that representatives now present make
definite suggestions as to the objectives of the Association
in order that these may be used by the Executive Committee in working up a draft.[11]

All the Committee's recommendations, including its nominations
for officers, were adopted, and the framework for building an organization was thus created.

Topics Addressed at Early Meetings

The topics of the addresses given at the first three meetings of the
American Association (1939, 1940, and 1941) offer an indication of
the primary concerns of business officers during those years. Such
concerns included accounting, budgeting, and financial reports, and
management of auxiliary enterprises, student labor, and physical
plant.

Accounting and Budgeting

The drive toward better and more uniform accounting practices
among all institutions of higher education, which later resulted in
publications such as *College & University Business Administration*
(NACUBO) and *Accounting for Colleges and Universities* (3rd ed.,
by Clarence Scheps and E.E. Davidson), had its genesis in the work
of men like Trevor Arnett, mentioned in Chapter 1; J. Harvey Cain,
of the American Council on Education's Financial Advisory Service;
and Thad L. Hungate, whose "Study of Financial Reports of Colleges
and Universities in the United States" was published in 1930 by the
National Committee on Standard Reports for Institutions of Higher
Education. Both Cain and Hungate were featured on the program of
American Association meetings in the early years. Another impor-

tant contributor to the improvement of accounting in higher education was Lloyd Morey, whose *University and College Accounting* was also published in 1930. Morey strongly influenced a generation of business officers at both white and black institutions.

In Cain's 1939 address, "Coordinating the Budget, the Accounting System, and the Financial Statement," he discussed the importance of the budget to a college or university, its relation to the institution's accounting system, the need for the financial statement to be comprehensible to its various publics such as governing boards, and the differences between accounting for commercial firms and for institutions of higher education. (Most business officers will agree that these concerns do not diminish in importance for institutions through the years.) Cain also presented in his talk a "Chart of Expenditures," which in its way was a forerunner of the model "Chart of Accounts" to be found in Part 5 of *College & University Business Administration* (NACUBO).

Accounting as applied to vocational education was the topic of an address by Edmund H. Burke, comptroller of Tuskegee Institute, at the 1939 meeting. For Tuskegee, which was heavily oriented to vocational education (the institution included divisions in carpentry, machine and welding, and printing, as well as a farm), an accounting system for the vocational areas was particularly important. Burke stressed the need for uniformity among institutions in accounting practices.

Also in 1939 Frank B. Adair, accountant at Arkansas A&M College, presented a talk on "Preparation of Uniform College Financial Reports." He referred to the National Committee on Standard Reports and emphasized the need for standardization of fiscal statements. It is evident from the three talks cited above that uniformity and standardization were becoming essential to good financial administration, and the men who planned the program for the American Association's first meeting felt it was important to make this point.

The interest in budgeting and fiscal affairs was also reflected in the program for 1940. J. Harvey Cain returned that year to speak on "Budget Preparation and Operation." Though institutions generally have become much more complex since Cain offered his suggestions to the American Association, what he said still holds true in the 1980s:

> Those who undertake the preparation of the budget . . .
> must be willing to study the needs of the institution as a
> whole, to give up petty schemes and proposals, to put

aside departmental jealousies so as to render no service for which the institution cannot pay. In other words, the preparation of a budget calls for teamwork of the highest order.[12]

A presentation on accounting problems and their solutions in the Atlanta University System was delivered at the 1940 meeting by Lucile Mack Strong, bursar of the system. This talk disclosed certain accounting problems (unique to a multiple-campus, consortium-like system) that had resulted from the affiliation of Atlanta University, Morehouse College, and Spelman College.

Student Labor

Student labor was an important part of campus life at most member institutions and its administration was emphasized in the Association's early programs. In 1939 three different addresses dealt with this subject: "Student Labor As Applied to Construction Work at Hampton Institute," by Robert O. Purves, treasurer, Hampton Institute; "Some Practices in the Employment of Student Labor," by J.H. Carter, business manager, Morgan State College; and "The Employment Service at Virginia Union," by L.W. Davis, personnel director, Virginia Union University.

In introducing his address, Purves commented that from the beginning of Hampton Institute, "honest labor, honestly performed, has been a basic thought and principle." He described the gradual development of curricula for the teaching of trades. "Work was performed in the saw mill, in the kitchens, on the farm, and in the sewing rooms, both from the viewpoint of 'learning by doing' and to earn funds with which to pay the board bill and to continue in school."[13]

In 1939, although Hampton Institute had grown in sophistication and had expanded its programs, the need to "learn by doing" and to "earn funds . . . to pay the board bill" was still of great importance. Purves's presentation explained the rationale by which students were graded, paid, and supervised. Carter's paper briefly described the practices then in common use regarding student labor, and noted that "supervision is the most difficult problem to solve."[14]

The employment service at Virginia Union University, as described by L.W. Davis, operated principally to find jobs for students off-campus where they could be of service to the community and earn much-needed funds for themselves. Such jobs involved basic tasks such as preparing an evening meal for a family, babysitting, domestic work, "odd jobs" of yard work or painting, or skilled work such as tutoring or typing.

Two papers given by Harold K. Logan, business manager of Wiley College, at the meetings in 1940 and 1941, respectively, also considered aspects of student employment. Logan's 1940 presentation gave a detailed account of on-campus jobs provided for students and his second talk focused on jobs for students as a form of financial aid.

National Youth Administration

It should be noted here that much of the work given to students at that time was funded by the National Youth Administration (NYA), which was created in 1935 as one of the New Deal organizations. This program provided funds for students as well as opportunities for them to perform services related to their educational objectives, and was a dependable source of income. Further, the required matching institutional contribution was relatively small. A committee of 32 persons had been appointed by President Roosevelt to formulate plans that resulted in the NYA. Among those persons were two prominent black educators, Mordecai W. Johnson, president of Howard University, and Mary McLeod Bethune, president of Bethune Cookman College.[15]

Auxiliary Enterprises

If space on the program indicated importance of subject matter, auxiliary enterprises rated high on the list for business officers in those first years of the new American Association. According to James B. Clarke, this may have been because various benefactors, such as foundations and government agencies, expected that students ought to take care of their living expenses so that funds designated for support of instruction would not be reduced. Auxiliaries that were discussed included bookstores, dining halls and cafeterias, residence halls, and student credit unions.

Caring for the health of students and providing them with pleasant surroundings in which to live and study were—and are—of great importance to business officers. From the addresses presented in the early years, it was evident that few such services were contracted out; they were managed and operated as an integral part of campus administration. Campus bookstores, too, were key: they were essential for supplying student textbooks, since in most cases there was nowhere else to purchase such books. Nevertheless, the possibility of stepping on the toes of local merchants by adding lines of merchandise that would attract more students to the campus bookstore was a concern, as it is in the 1980s.

Physical Plant

The operation and maintenance of physical plant were also of great interest to business officers at those early meetings. Each year— 1939, 1940, and 1941—featured an address on some aspect of physical plant. In 1939 Edward S. Hope, superintendent of physical plant at Howard University, spoke about the university's new power plant and distribution system; "Planning Useful and Economical School Buildings" was presented in 1940 by Louis E. Fry, architect at Tuskegee Institute; and in 1941 an address on the operation and maintenance of physical plant was given by H.H. Linn, superintendent of buildings and grounds at Teachers College, New York City.

Other Subjects

A range of other subjects was treated on the programs of the Association's first years, including insurance, the operation of a college farm, purchasing, student aid, and social security. A brief presentation on the last was prepared for the 1939 meeting by Rainard B. Robbins, vice president and actuary of the Teachers Insurance and Annuity Association (TIAA), in the expectation that social security would shortly be extended to cover nonprofit institutions such as colleges and universities; in fact, the extension did not take place and Robbins used most of his time to talk about TIAA insurance. He predicted, however, that churches and colleges would eventually unite to have their exemption from social security lifted, so that they could reap some benefits from the general taxation associated with the social security program.

Funding Black Education

The problem of financial support for black education was treated at length at the 1939 meeting and was also featured, in connection with particular states, at the 1940 and 1941 meetings.

Doxey A. Wilkerson, associate professor of education at Howard University, spoke in 1939 on the "Allocation of Public Funds for Higher Education among Negroes," which dealt principally with the 17 black land-grant colleges in the South.

An imposing group of experts joined forces in 1939 to present papers on the general topic of "Financial Support of Higher Education among Negroes." Those speakers were Mordecai W. Johnson, president of Howard University; John W. Davis, president of West Virginia State College; Jackson Davis, associate director of the General Education Board; and Fred J. Kelly, chief of the United States Office of Education (which was then a part of the Department of the Interior). Johnson's presentation dealt with general conditions in the South; he mentioned the poverty of the land itself, and the struggles of both whites and blacks to make it yield a fair living, and commented, especially in regard to other sections of the country, that ". . . the long continuance of the Depression has made some of our most realistic and able men see that if something could be done to raise the buying power of that third of the nation that live in the South, it would have a great deal to do with the health of this entire nation."[16] He also suggested that business officers had much to offer in terms of helping colleges and universities provide the best possible education with the funds available.

John W. Davis suggested in his address that the place to begin financial support for higher education for blacks was in the institutions themselves. He also recommended a ". . . self-study program for colleges which would lead to more substantial financial well-being." Such a self-study, he said, would promote "a working knowledge of the items which are considered in determining the adequacy of financial support of an educational institution."[17] Among such items he included expenditure per student for educational purposes, institutional dependence on student fees, stability of financing, indebtedness, and accounting procedures.

Comments by Jackson Davis at the 1939 meeting formed a short summary of the help given to black colleges by the General Education Board, and Fred Kelly spoke briefly on a study—planned by the federal government—of higher education institutions.

In 1940 Horace Mann Bond, president of Fort Valley State College, spoke on the "Support of Public Higher Education in Alabama, 1865-1930," and in 1941 Dallas C. Brown, director of business administration at West Virginia State College, presented an address on the "Financial History of Higher Education for Negroes in West Virginia." Both papers showed evidence of painstaking research. Their contents make somber reading. Some advances had been made by 1939 in the area of higher education for blacks, but the limitations on funding were, in effect, crippling and the prospect of change did not appear bright. Thus, financial support—or the lack of it—was a principal concern of business officers in the early years of the American Association.

Problems of the Business Officer

In 1941 V.D. Johnston addressed his colleagues on the problems that he perceived to be "immediately ahead" of the business officer.[18] He related those problems basically to enrollment (and mentioned the increased enrollment in black colleges that undoubtedly would result from the growing number of public secondary schools for blacks). Cited were a shift in enrollment toward more state-supported institutions of higher education; the necessity to meet changed enrollment with adequate physical plant; the need to pay greater attention to campus grounds and the appearance of buildings (to attract students and favorably impress their families); the need for increases in the size of the business office staff and for well-trained business personnel to meet the demands of a growing enrollment for more services; the need for better and more cooperative purchasing; and the need for greater attention to investments. Institutions had clearly begun to change radically from the days when a college president could keep records in his desk drawer. The function of the college or university business officer was expanding on all fronts and the American Association would help its members to meet the challenge.

Second Meeting—1940

Tuskegee Institute was selected from among several institutions that offered to host the American Association's second meeting, which was held on March 28-30, 1940. Tuskegee Institute was founded in 1881 as an agricultural and mechanical school for blacks, and its famous first president, Booker T. Washington, has become an American legend. A story about the founding of Tuskegee was related by Horace Mann Bond in the 1940 Proceedings:

> In 1880 came the third establishment of a state-supported institution for Negroes. As Emmett Scott has told it, "It came about that in the year 1880 in Macon County, Alabama, a certain ex-Confederate colonel conceived the idea that if he could secure the Negro vote he could beat his rival and win the seat he coveted in the state legislature. Accordingly, the colonel went to the leading Negro in the town of Tuskegee, and asked him what he could do to secure the Negro vote, for Negroes then voted in Alabama without restriction. This man, Lewis Adams by name, himself an ex-slave, promptly replied that what the

> race most wanted was education, and that what they most
> needed was industrial education, and that if he (the colo-
> nel) would agree to work for the passage of a bill appro-
> priating money for the maintenance of an industrial school
> for Negroes, he (Adams) would help to get for him the
> Negro vote and the election. This bargain between an ex-
> slaveholder and an ex-slave was made and faithfully ob-
> served on both sides, with the result that the following
> year the legislature of Alabama appropriated $2,000 a year
> for the establishment of a normal and industrial school
> for Negroes in the town of Tuskegee."[19]

Lloyd Isaacs was treasurer of Tuskegee Institute at the time of the
1940 meeting.

The "Purpose" of the newly formed Association was printed in
the Proceedings for 1940:

> To secure closer association personally and for our insti-
> tutions, for discussion of mutual problems, and to secure
> the advancement of professional standards among those
> responsible for the business administration of the insti-
> tutions that serve Negroes.[20]

Membership qualifications were also listed; they were described
as "very informal. Any institution doing the work of a Junior College
and above may become a member by payment of the fee of ten dollars
annually."[21] Membership entitled an institution to unlimited representation at the annual meetings and one free copy of the Proceedings.

Five new members were added to the American Association in
1940: Clark College, Atlanta, Georgia; Langston University, Langston, Oklahoma; Philander Smith College, Little Rock, Arkansas;
Talladega College, Talladega, Alabama; and Tougaloo College, Tougaloo, Mississippi (see Appendix 3 for a complete list of all institutions that were at some time a member of the American Association). It was evident that the presence of the young organization
was being felt in other ways as well: it designated Frank B. Adair of
Arkansas AM&N College as its representative to an August meeting
of the American Teachers Association and named Luther H. Foster,
Jr., budget officer at Howard University, as the American Association
delegate to an April meeting of the American Negro Conference.

On recommendation from the Executive Committee, it was
determined that the Association's fiscal year should extend from

July 1 to June 30. The appointment of two new committees was announced at the 1940 business meeting: one to audit the treasurer's accounts and one to handle nominations, meetings, and resolutions. (Registration for the 1940 meeting involved an outlay of only $2.50, and the charge for the banquet was $1.50 per participant.)

The financial statement for the period April 23, 1939, to March 29, 1940, was read in the report of the Auditing Committee. Receipts from the annual dues of 43 institutions, reprints of special articles (perhaps addresses given at the 1939 meeting), and sale of 11 copies of the 1939 Proceedings totaled $496.75 (one free copy of the Proceedings had been given to each member). Disbursements—mostly for printing and postage—amounted to $452.50. Thus, the American Association entered its second year of existence with a cash balance of $44.25.

Because of the desirability of policy continuity in the early stages of association life, the Committee on Nominations, Meetings, and Resolutions suggested that the Association's officers be retained for one more year. It also recommended that fewer topics be on the programs in order to allow more time for discussion, and that permanent dates be set by the Executive Committee for future meetings.

As in 1939, several institutions offered to host the next meeting. The site chosen was Bluefield State Teachers College, in Bluefield, West Virginia.

Third Meeting—1941

Bluefield State Teachers College was established in 1865 as the second state-supported institution for black higher education in West Virginia.[22] President H.L. Dickason of Bluefield welcomed the American Association to its third meeting, May 8-10, 1941.

One of the first actions at the 1941 meeting was to divide the Committee on Nominations, Meetings, and Resolutions into three separate committees: one on Time and Place of Meeting, one on Resolutions, and one on Nominations. The Auditing Committee was retained as previously organized. New members were appointed for each committee.

At the business meeting three new Association members were approved: Meharry Medical College, Nashville, Tennessee; Morehouse College, Atlanta, Georgia; and Voorhees N&I, Denmark, South Carolina.

The treasurer's report was presented by Charles R. Rutherford of West Virginia State College. When disbursements of $437.80 had been subtracted from receipts totaling $552.20, the Association was left with a balance of $114.40, or more than twice as much as at the end of the previous fiscal year.

Several recommendations were made by the Executive Committee, including one to send a telegram of appreciation and goodwill to Trevor Arnett, president emeritus of the General Education Board, in recognition of his many years of service to black education. The committee further recommended approval by the Association of a proposed amendment to social security legislation to provide old age and unemployment benefits for employees of educational institutions.

Finally, the committee recommended that officers and members of the American Association gather information on various means of providing student aid (scholarships, tuition remission, student labor, and others) for use in a survey of scholarships and student aid proposed by Thad L. Hungate and John W. Davis.

The Committee on Nominations, while acknowledging the "able leadership" of the Association's officers, indicated agreement with the president, L.H. Foster, Sr., that "it will be a desirable policy . . . to rotate the positions within the membership."[23] (See Appendix 4 for a complete list of officers for all years of the Association's existence.)

Placement Officer

One other important nomination was made: L.H. Foster, Sr., was named placement officer of the Association. The position of placement officer, unique to the American Association (none of the other organizations of business officers had such a post), was created to ensure the continuation of Foster's previous, informal efforts to place promising young black graduates in administrative positions at black colleges. The need for a formal mechanism by which institutions could find qualified candidates for business or financial jobs and by which persons interested in such jobs could be hired prompted establishment of this key position, which was to remain a part of the organization until the Association's dissolution.

The Association voted to accept an invitation from David D. Jones, president of Bennett College in Greensboro, North Carolina, to host the next annual meeting, to be held on May 7-9, 1942. Before that meeting took place, Pearl Harbor would be bombed and the United States would be at war. World War II would create additional problems for business officers at black colleges just as it would for those at all institutions in the country—but it would also open up new, unexpected opportunities for black students and broaden the scope of administration at their schools.

References—Chapter 2

1. Margaret D. Welch, interview with author.
2. Ibid.
3. Rayford A. Logan and Michael R. Winston, *The Dictionary of American Negro Biography* (New York: W.W. Norton, 1982).
4. Arthur Paul Davis, interview with author.
5. Resume provided by Lucius Wyatt, Hampton Institute.
6. Material provided by Robert D. Carroll, Florida A&M University.
7. Walter Dyson, *Howard University: The Capstone of Negro Education, 1867-1940* (Washington, DC: Graduate School of Howard University, 1941).
8. Ibid.
9. Doxey A. Wilkerson, Howard University, "Allocation of Public Funds for Higher Education among Negroes," 1939 Proceedings.
10. Material provided by James B. Clarke.
11. 1939 Proceedings, pp. 14-15.
12. J. Harvey Cain, American Council on Education, "Budget Preparation and Operation," 1939 Proceedings, p. 101.
13. Robert O. Purves, Hampton Institute, "Student Labor As Applied to Construction Work at Hampton Institute," 1939 Proceedings, p. 28.
14. James H. Carter, Morgan State College, "Some Practices in the Employment of Student Labor," 1939 Proceedings, p. 34.
15. Leland Stanford Cozart, *History of the Association of Colleges and Secondary Schools, 1934-1965* (Charlotte, NC: Heritage Printer, 1964).
16. Mordecai W. Johnson, Howard University, address, 1939 Proceedings, p. 69.
17. John W. Davis, West Virginia State College, "Financial Support of Higher Education among Negroes," 1939 Proceedings, p. 72.
18. V.D. Johnston, Howard University, "Some Problems Immediately Ahead of the Business Officer," 1941 Proceedings, p. 35.
19. Horace Mann Bond, Fort Valley State College, "Support of Public Higher Education in Alabama, 1865-1930," 1940 Proceedings, p. 39.
20. 1940 Proceedings, p. 8.
21. Ibid.

22. Dallas C. Brown, West Virginia State College, "Financial History of Higher Education for Negroes in West Virginia," 1941 Proceedings.

23. 1941 Proceedings, pp. 17-18.

3

Coping with a World War: 1942-1945

World War II was undoubtedly the most important influence in the affairs of colleges and universities from 1942 to 1945. For members of the American Association, the war meant the same kinds of constraints and hardships that were imposed on their white counterparts, but it also brought with it certain opportunities, such as the pilot training program at Tuskegee Institute and the naval installation at Hampton Institute. Many challenges for business officers grew out of such programs and out of the war itself, intensifying the need for the American Association and the professional assistance it could offer.

Topics Discussed in Meetings of the War Years

National Defense

As might be expected, national defense and its influence on predominantly black institutions of higher education were primary subjects for discussion at American Association meetings during the war years, especially in 1942, when the country was mobilizing on all fronts to gear a peacetime economy for war.

At the beginning of his 1942 talk entitled "Our Institutions in National Defense," W.A. Hamilton, former head of business training at Virginia State College and the business manager at Lincoln University of Missouri, succinctly described the situation in America concerning the defense industry:

> In the present crisis, the nation has declared itself dedi-
> cated to an "all-out-for-defense" program. In addition to
> the expansion of the armed forces, we have assumed the
> major responsibility for the production of war materials
> for the united nations engaged in the fight for the pres-
> ervation of democracy. The training of men and women
> for employment in defense industries constitutes an es-
> sential prerequisite to the increased production of these
> supplies. The responsibility for this training has been placed
> upon the schools and colleges. Realizing the expectation
> placed upon them to prepare citizens for worthwhile life
> situations—at present, preparation for war—the schools
> have accepted the challenge.[1]

The address stated that as early as June 1940, Congress had appropriated $15 million for an "extensive vocational program"[2] to
prepare workers for defense industries; in October of that same year,
another $60 million had been appropriated for this purpose. The
vocational education program was administered by the U. S. Office
of Education, under the provisions of several laws, through state
boards for vocational education and universities and colleges.

The program was divided into various areas of training, designed
partly to offer refresher courses to persons who already had some
relevant training but especially to give instruction in areas necessary
to the defense industry, such as mechanics, engineering, and chemistry. A bill passed by Congress in 1941 gathered several areas together under the rubric "engineering, science, and management defense training," or ESMDT. The objective of ESMDT was to provide
specific college-level short courses in needed areas, but it was not
intended to be a general college program.[3]

Federal funds were available to qualified colleges and universities
that wished to participate in ESMDT. Qualifications included the
capability of providing degrees in "engineering, chemistry, physics,
or production supervision" at the completion of a four-year course
of study.[4] The traditionally black institutions were eager to cooperate in supplying instruction for the national defense, though the
still strongly entrenched problem of racial bias hindered even this
urgent cause. As stated by W.A. Hamilton:

> What resources are made available to Negroes under the
> defense training program? The acts named above specify
> that "no trainee shall be discriminated against because of
> sex, race or color and where separate schools are required

by law for separate population groups, to the extent needed
for trainees of each such group, equitable provisions shall
be made for facilities and training of like quality."

Contrary to the stated policy, the administrative councils
for vocational training in some of the states having separate schools have found loopholes to evade the law. The
council in one such state recently passed a resolution that
no courses would be provided for Negroes unless there
was first a demand on the part of prospective employers
of Negro personnel. In another state, some defense courses
for Negroes were held up because qualified and experienced Negro teachers were unavailable. It was planned to
employ white instructors for the Negro trainees. However,
the attorney general rendered an opinion that the provisions of the state law make it unlawful for instructors of
one race to teach pupils of the other in the public schools.
Thus in the preparation for the defense of democracy, the
Negro is again caught in a vicious circle.

In spite of these barriers, our schools have faith in free-
dom's cause. Even though federal funds are not made available to all schools, the curricula of most of our institutions
have been enriched to include courses in defense training.[5]

A survey of black colleges, the results of which were included in
Hamilton's paper, indicated that of 38 member institutions replying
(out of a possible 48), 30 were offering defense courses. Of those 30,
21 were receiving government aid—the other 17 making defense
courses available through their own resources.[6] From this it can be
seen that black Americans felt a strong responsibility to aid in the
war effort and were not to be deterred by the strictures of a narrow
social tradition.

Blake R. Van Leer, dean of engineering, North Carolina State College, discussed the ESMDT program at length in his address on that
topic at the 1942 American Association meeting, and Jesse F. Beals,
comptroller of Fisk University, spoke briefly on "Winning the Peace,"
in which he suggested four ways for colleges to help the war effort:

1. Build up a reserve to compensate for falling attendance
    and declining income.

2. Purchase in conservative fashion any supplies that have
    advanced to higher price levels.

3. Use substitute materials to replace those designated
   for vital war needs.

4. Keep the curriculum flexible to accommodate possible
   changes that will be brought about by peace.[7]

It is interesting to note that Beals's fourth topic already looks toward
the end of the war.

The next address that dealt with the war effort was presented at
the 1945 American Association meeting by Colonel Jay Dykhouse,
chief of the Pre-Induction Training Branch of the Eighth Service
Command, Dallas, Texas. The purpose of Dykhouse's address was
to emphasize ways in which colleges and universities could help
prepare young men and boys for the training they would receive in
the Army. Such preparation included physical training and instruction in certain mechanical areas, including the machine shop. Dykhouse pointed out that because of the lowering of the draft age, the
armed services were no longer getting men who, when drafted, already had necessary skills.

Tuskegee Institute and the Army Air Corps

World War II introduced new technologies and opened up fields
of knowledge that were to have profound influence, ranging from
the so-called "miracle" drugs, such as penicillin, to the awe-inspiring
advances in rocketry and the use of atomic energy. For blacks the
war acted as a catalyst to speed up social changes that in other
circumstances might have required much more time to accomplish,
or that perhaps would not have happened at all. The development
of an Army Air Corps pilot training program at Tuskegee Institute
was a case in point.

In an interview for this history, Colonel (ret.) Herbert E. Carter,
a member of Tuskegee Airmen, Inc., commented, "Before 1941 the
attitude of the white majority was that black people simply did not
have the ability to do anything as complicated as flying an aircraft."
This was in spite of such early black aviation pioneers as Bessie
Coleman, who became a pilot in 1922, and James Herman Banning
and Thomas C. Allen, who in 1932 were the first blacks to make a
transcontinental flight.[8]

In 1939 blacks were admitted to the Civilian Pilot Training Program (CPT) established by the Civil Aeronautics Authority,[9] and six
black colleges were named to participate: Howard University, Delaware State College, Hampton Institute, North Carolina A&T, West
Virginia State College, and Tuskegee Institute.[10] After the bombing

of Pearl Harbor, a War Training Service Program (WTS)[11] was started and Tuskegee Institute was chosen as the site for the training of black aviators (the all-black 99th Pursuit Squadron had been activated in March 1941). Two airfields were used: Moton Air Field, operated by Tuskegee Institute at that time and now serving the town of Tuskegee, and a new installation built by the Army Air Corps and abandoned after the war.[12]

An estimated 2,000 black aviators had received their wings by the end of the war, nearly all of them graduates of the program at Tuskegee Institute.[13] They had earned acclaim for their skill as fighters and had been sought after by white bomber crews as escorts because of their excellent record of protecting the larger planes.[14] In May 1949 the all-black units were dissolved as a result of President Truman's July 1948 decree announcing a new policy of racial integration of the armed forces.

Naval Installation at Hampton Institute

In May 1942 it was announced at Hampton Institute that the institution had been designated by the secretary of the navy, and approved by the President of the United States, as the "first school of its kind for the training of Negro enlisted personnel as specialists in many skills in order that they might qualify for petty officer ratings."[15] The first group of officers and enlisted men to be graduated from the resulting Naval Training School began the program the following September. The unit was under the command of Edwin H. Downs, USNR.

The first Negro petty officers to enter the U.S. Navy in World War II, a company of 128 men, were graduated from the Training School on January 2, 1943. The Navy provided some facilities (including a swimming pool and recreation center), and certain residence halls and other facilities already belonging to the Institute were designated for the use of the Navy trainees. In addition to the petty officers, many other students, both men and women, were trained as electrician's mates, machinist's mates, carpenter's mates, metalsmiths, shipfitters, coxswains, and cooks and bakers. Altogether, nearly 5,000 students went through the Training School. The closing exercises of the last graduating class took place in August 1945, days before Japan accepted surrender terms and World War II ended.

Hampton Institute was also involved with U.S. Army training, including a Reserve Officers' Training Corps, an Ordnance Training Detachment, and an Army Specialized Training Unit. Further, a number of men in the elementary flight training course at Hampton were sent to Tuskegee Institute to participate in advanced pilot training.[16]

Other War-Related Topics

"The Effect of the War on Negro Education" was presented at the 1944 American Association meeting by Henry G. Badger, associate specialist in educational statistics, U.S. Office of Education. As well as mentioning certain decreases in the numbers of students and teachers, no doubt a result of more persons entering both the armed forces and war-related industries, Badger had some interesting comments to make about the financial condition of Negro schools. Problems with budgets indicated a general state of confusion in the economy of the country. He suggested that institutions should encourage financial contributions to education, because there was more money in circulation than there had been for many years. In addition, Badger spoke of the need to begin building up student aid funds "so as to take care of the student who is going to need an education when the war boom is over and money is not so abundant."[17]

Postwar Planning

Members of the American Association were already thinking ahead to the dramatic changes in higher education that they realized would occur once World War II had ended. Presentations at both the 1944 and the 1945 meetings addressed this concern.

In 1944 William M. Cooper, who for many years directed the summer school program at Hampton Institute, spoke on "Reorganizing and Adapting the College Curriculum to Meet Postwar Needs of Soldiers, War Workers, and Youth in General." He pointed out the considerable differences in degrees of maturity between, on the one hand, the normal beginning student fresh from high school and, on the other, the soldier who had endured great hardships or the industrial worker who had learned responsibility and independence under the pressure of intense war work. These three kinds of persons would have to be accommodated. In addition to adapting the academic curriculum, the institutions would probably need to provide counseling and guidance. All such adaptations and/or additions, of course, had serious financial implications for member institutions of the American Association.

In the 1945 meeting, anticipated postwar issues were discussed under two specific titles: "Postwar Building Planning," by G. Leon Netterville, business manager, Southern University, and "The Veterans Education Program," by Durrell A. Hiller, chief of the Vocational Rehabilitation and Education Division, Veterans Administration, New Orleans, Louisiana. Netterville's talk was brief, to allow for discussion from the floor. One of the more prophetic comments offered was that by Wendell G. Morgan, business manager, Johnson C. Smith College: "It will be of some value to give some thought to the postwar problem of returning veterans who are married. . . . They are already separated from their families and do not feel that they wish to continue so. Will we give any thought to providing quarters for married couples?"[18] It was evident that the face of traditional higher education was to be greatly changed.

In his talk Hiller stated that at that time (May 1945) more than 1,500,000 veterans had been discharged from the armed forces; he further noted that "at the end of hostilities, anywhere from ten to twelve million persons . . . will be returned to civilian life."[19] Hiller discussed the need for vocational rehabilitation, counseling, and education and training, and outlined what would have to be done to carry out these steps. He explained that "the policy of the Veterans Administration is to utilize the recognized colleges, universities, junior colleges, business and commercial schools, trade and industrial schools, business establishments, and industrial firms and farms . . . as a means of accomplishing the vocational rehabilitation of disabled veterans."[20] Hiller ended with a brief description of what has become one of the best-known pieces of legislation ever enacted by Congress: the Servicemen's Readjustment Act of 1944, or "the G.I. Bill of Rights."

United Negro College Fund

A concept of major importance to black institutions was realized in 1944 with the first campaign of the United Negro College Fund (UNCF). Until that time, it will be remembered, outside support for private black colleges came principally from individual private donors and missionary and church groups, and later from such foundations as the General Education Board and the Julius Rosenwald Fund. But various private sources were beginning to dry up, and separate fund-raising drives on the part of individual institutions, which had little money to spend on publicity and campaigns, were not very effective. An increased need for additional funds, brought on by the accelerated interest in higher education, made this problem critical.

W.J. Trent, Jr., executive secretary of the UNCF, described the origins and operation of the Fund and presented the hopes and plans of its organizers at the 1944 meeting of the American Association.

He explained that "two foundations, the General Education Board and the Julius Rosenwald Fund, underwrote one-half of the cost of the campaign."[21] Though F.D. Patterson, president of Tuskegee Institute, was largely responsible for the concept of the UNCF, the idea for pooling the resources of black institutions to achieve better fund-raising results had been mentioned by V.D. Johnston at the 1941 meeting of the American Association:

> If a moment can be found when some one of the private schools in our Association is not conducting its own campaign, there should be a possibility for a united campaign for scholarship funds that would be centrally conducted. Even if only six, eight, or ten of the private schools cooperated in a campaign solely for scholarship and loan funds for worthy students, thought of the appeal opens a vista that warrants examination. . . . An appeal to give money to aid worthy, needy students is not one that can be easily refused. There are many evident advantages in the plan for a large, united campaign. . . . With a pooling of resources of alumni, and philanthropy, the duplication of effort, the competition, advertising, travel, correspondence and similar costs would be reduced, almost in proportion to the number of schools cooperating. Such a campaign could have educational force among the alumni, with cumulative results that few of our schools have explored.[22]

The United Negro College Fund was discussed again in 1945 by Luther H. Foster, Jr., then treasurer of Tuskegee Institute. He explained that at the time there were 32 members of the Fund, which was administered by a control group and an executive committee (the latter consisted of 13 delegates chosen from among the 32 members). Although there was still some discussion of how to divide equitably the money received from the Fund campaign, Foster suggested that the existence of the Fund and the institutional cooperation on which it depended were both significant advances for black colleges.

Review of the Gaines Decision

At the Association's 1944 meeting, a notable presentation, important not only for its application to blacks in that year but for its significance as a portent of things to come, was "A Review of the Application of the Gaines Decision," by Leon A. Ransom, professor of law, Howard University. The thrust of Ransom's address was to dispel euphemistic notions that the decision reached by the Supreme Court in *Missouri ex rel Gaines* v. *Canada* had marked a "new signpost on the road to racial equality and true democracy."[23]

The Gaines decision involved a black college graduate, Lloyd Gaines, who wished to study law and who had challenged Missouri state legislation that provided for a fund to educate blacks outside the state in those professions for which there were no facilities for blacks inside the state. Although the Court declared in its decision that a state must provide equal educational facilities for all its citizens regardless of race—thus striking down the notion that a citizen could be "exiled" outside the state to study a professional course offered to other citizens within the state—it did not deny the "separate but equal" doctrine. To quote Ransom:

> The Court concluded by repeating the old doctrine, which, as I have said before, is obviously fallacious, that the duty to educate equally within the state did not necessarily require education in the same institution.[24]

Ransom continued by pointing out that there were only two important departures from established doctrine in this case—one that negated the idea of substituting scholarships for instruction within the state, and another that asserted that educational opportunities must be individual rather than collective. He added that, because of the two departures noted above, states were left to choose among four alternatives:

1. To admit Negroes to the state universities in courses not offered in the state schools for Negroes.
2. To duplicate, immediately upon demand, in the state schools for Negroes the courses of instruction given at the institutions for white citizens.
3. To absorb, by outright purchase or by contract, the facilities afforded within the state to Negroes by privately owned or operated institutions, and thus inferentially make such institutions adjuncts of the state for Negro education.
4. To pool their resources and set up "regional universities" which would be supported jointly by the several states within the region and would thus be equally available to all the Negro applicants from the several states.[25]

Ransom then examined each of the four proposals and showed that the only one to be both legal and practical was the first, which was, in fact, adopted by West Virginia. Ransom concluded that this choice:

> . . . means the end of segregation and discrimination. But more important to us, it means the beginning of the end of the dual school system under which we now operate and for whose maintenance we meet here, however reluctantly, today. *Are we as Negro educators willing and courageous enough to admit that we are gradually working ourselves out of the American picture as a separate racial group and willing to sacrifice personal ambitions for group achievements?* [emphasis added] This is "the sixty-four dollar question" which started with the Gaines decision and which we must now answer.[26]

Without doubt, the question addressed to "Negro educators" was as pointed for those in administration as for those on the faculty.

Other Topics

Two presentations at the 1942 Association meeting addressed the subject of black higher education in North Carolina: "Financial History of State Institutions of Higher Education for Negroes in North Carolina," by N.C. Newbold, state department of education in Raleigh, and "The Present Status of Higher Education among Negroes in North Carolina," by Nelson H. Harris, director of teacher training, Shaw University. An encouraging note for black education in North Carolina was sounded by Harris, who stated that "in 1921 there were 4,196 teachers in Negro schools of the state, and the average training of these teachers was below the high school graduation level."[27] But in 1939-1940, according to Harris, statistics showed that "the training of Negro teachers was just slightly less than one-fourth of a year below that of white teachers."[28] Harris added that this was especially remarkable when one considered that "graduate study facilities have only been available within the state to any extent for Negroes since 1939."[29]

Papers on black education in other states had been presented in the earlier meetings of the Association. However, no similar presentations were made after 1942, until 1947. A growing concern with mobilization for war and later with returned veterans seems to have taken the place of more regional subjects.

The topics of retirement and social security occupied much of the program at the 1942 meeting. Charles L. Franklin, of the Social Security Board, Washington, DC, spoke on the "Present Status of Social Security Legislation Affecting Institutions of Higher Education." He described the provisions of the Social Security Act and those entities exempt from the act—including nonprofit organizations such as colleges and universities—adding that "methods are being developed to extend the protection of the program to employees of nonprofit institutions without endangering the institutions' general tax-exempt status."[30]

Retirement options for state employees in Virginia and in North Carolina were presented in addresses by Louis H. Schuster, Virginia State College, and Andrew I. Terrell, business manager, Winston-Salem Teachers College. Schuster's comments on the Virginia plan indicated that the state had been somewhat behind in looking after its public servants in their old age, regardless of color, but that with the 1942 Virginia Retirement Act a positive step had been taken to correct the situation. Near the end of his address Schuster commented, "I searched the act with diligence for evidence of anti-Negro references, but I am happy to say my search was fruitless. The law makes no references whatsoever to Negroes, nor does it provide for separate annuity tables for Negro and white employees."[31] Thus, an inkling of later progress between the races could already be seen in certain legislation. According to Terrell's address on North Carolina, that state's retirement system was established in July 1941 and provided an automatic savings plan for its state employees.

That the "sphere of influence" of the black institution was widening was reflected at the 1942 meeting in two addresses on the subject of public relations. Those talks dealt with the aspects of public relations that continue to be important to any institution: the need to become known to relevant publics, the need for favorable publicity, and the problems of financing the public relations effort.

A growing awareness of the importance of the business officer and the administration of finance was evident in two other talks presented in 1942: one, by W.C. Jackson, dean of the Women's College of the University of North Carolina, discussed "The Total College" and the place of good business administration in this concept, and the other, "The Business Office as Classroom," by David D. Jones, president of Bennett College, pointed out the need for administrators to be as aware as faculty members of "teaching" the campus community by their example and quality of work.

Topics discussed at the 1945 meeting, in addition to those already described, indicated that with the end of World War II in sight, administrators were once again thinking along more normal lines in their perceptions of duties and problems. Topics included "Principles of Accounting and Finance," by Clarence Scheps, then supervisor of finance for the state department of education, Baton Rouge, Louisiana, and "The Development and Administration of Student Loan Funds," by James B. Clarke, assistant comptroller, Hampton Institute. The former presented the basic concerns of business officers regarding accounting, while the latter looked ahead to a time of higher student enrollment and greater interest in obtaining loans for education.

Fourth Meeting—1942

Although national defense occupied an important position on the program of the 1942 meeting, nothing in the minutes of that meeting refers to the entrance of the United States into active combat in World War II. However, the Committee on Nominations, perhaps reflecting a need for stability, recommended that the same officers be retained for another year—with two new persons, J.V. Anderson, Bishop College, and Charles C. Amey, North Carolina College for Negroes, to be added to the Executive Committee.

A table attached to the minutes showed student fees at member institutions for the academic year 1941-1942. A similar table, for the preceding academic year, had been attached to the minutes for the 1941 meeting and this practice was continued for other meetings through 1946, indicating the interest of institutional representatives in comparing such statistics.

Bennett College for Women hosted the 1942 meeting on May 7-9. Almore M. Dale, a product of Tuskegee Institute's program in business, was business manager of Bennett when the American Association convened the meeting.

Fifth Meeting—1944

In the closing paragraphs of the 1942 minutes, it was stated that the next annual meeting of the American Association was planned for May 6-8, 1943, at Hampton Institute. In fact, the fifth meeting took place at the designated site on June 8-9, 1944. No explanation is given for having skipped a year, but it is not hard to discern a reason in the limitations imposed by war, which made it difficult both to feed visitors and to travel (certain foods and gasoline were rationed, and members of the armed services received priority on public modes of transportation).

Hampton Institute, which became Hampton University in 1985, is one of the oldest traditionally black institutions in the United States. The beginnings of Hampton Institute, under General Samuel Chapman Armstrong, are described by Robert O. Purves, treasurer of the Institute, as follows:

> At the end of the Civil War, when Gen. Armstrong was sent by the Freedmen's Bureau to Hampton, he found a most distressing situation and a gigantic problem. Between six and seven thousand Negro refugees, who had fled from various parts of the South, had gathered in that vicinity for the protection which might be afforded them by the Federal troops which were massed in large numbers at Fort Monroe and adjacent territory. It will be remembered that Fort Monroe was the only fort in the Southern states that remained in the hands of Federal troops throughout the Civil War.
>
> This great crowd of refugees was completely dependent upon "Uncle Sam." They were destitute and without shelter or substance of any kind. Gen. Armstrong, as an agent of the Government, attacked the immediate problem of providing what shelter was possible in old army barracks and of rationing food and clothing. For some months he headed up this work of emergency relief but increasingly realized the enormous problem confronting these newly emancipated freedmen, a problem which he recognized was a national responsibility to face and help. The development of opportunities for economic betterment and the creation of new living conditions were the great objectives.
>
> And so Gen. Armstrong in 1868 began a modest little school, beginning on the level and in the fields most useful to the people he was dedicating his life to serve. To strengthen the economic footing of the race and to develop intellectual powers were his purposes, but with the greatest emphasis on, and belief in, the spiritual life for all people.[32]

The fifth meeting was shorter than the others and fewer speakers and topics were presented. As in 1942, this time with specific reference to the "chaotic conditions existing at this time,"[33] the same officers were retained, with one exception: Jesse F. Beals, who had been vice president, was no longer in higher education, and it was recommended that his successor be A.H. Turner of St. Paul's Polytechnic Institute, Lawrenceville, Virginia. It was further recommended that L.H. Foster, Sr., who had been named president of Virginia State College, should be retained as placement officer because he had maintained "profound interest in the Association" even though he was no longer a business officer.[34]

Sixth Meeting—1945

The host of the 1945 American Association meeting was Southern University, Scotlandville, Louisiana (the address later became Baton Rouge). Southern University was started in New Orleans in 1881 and was recognized in 1892 as a land-grant college under the Second Morrill Act. In 1912 the university plant in New Orleans was sold and the institution was moved to Scotlandville, where it opened in 1914 on Scott's Bluff on the Mississippi River.

The university expanded in 1956 and again in 1964, when the Louisiana legislature created branches of the institution in New Orleans and Shreveport. In 1975 the Southern University System was created and a system office was established.

The sixth meeting began with a report from the president, Don A. Davis, who welcomed two new members—Spelman College, Atlanta, Georgia, and Storer College, Harpers Ferry, West Virginia. Davis noted that he had recently attended a meeting of the Eastern Association of College and University Business Officers, together with two other members of the Association. For the first time in several years, new officers were recommended by the Committee on Nominations.

The minutes of an Executive Committee meeting were included in the 1945 Proceedings of the American Association meeting. The committee meeting, which had taken place in January, dealt with topics to be presented at the 1945 annual meeting. One interesting statement from the committee session illustrates the constraints brought on by wartime: "The committee was of the opinion that less than 50 persons would have to use the railroad to attend the meeting in Scotlandville so that no application need be made to the Office of Defense Transportation."[35]

With the next American Association meeting, in the spring of 1946, World War II would be over and institutions everywhere would be feeling the impact of a new and urgent demand for higher education.

References—Chapter 3

1. W.A. Hamilton, Lincoln University (Missouri), "Our Institutions in National Defense," 1942 Proceedings, p. 54.
2. Ibid.
3. Blake R. Van Leer, North Carolina State College, "The Engineering, Science, and Management Defense Training Program," 1942 Proceedings.
4. Ibid.
5. Hamilton, "Our Institutions in National Defense," 1942 Proceedings, p. 55.
6. Ibid., pp. 55-56.
7. Jesse F. Beals, Fisk University, "Winning the Peace," 1942 Proceedings, p. 67.
8. Von Hardesty and Dominick Pisano, *Black Wings: The American Black in Aviation* (Washington, DC: Smithsonian Institution, 1983).
9. Ibid., p. 19.
10. Robert A. Rose, *Lonely Eagles: The Story of America's Black Air Force in World War II* (Tuskegee Western Airmen, Inc., Western Region), p. 11.
11. Hardesty and Pisano, *Black Wings*, p. 21.
12. Colonel (ret.) Herbert E. Carter, interview with author.
13. Hardesty and Pisano, *Black Wings*, p. 21.
14. Carter, interview with author.
15. Walter R. Brown, Hampton Institute, remarks at closing exercises of U.S. Naval Training School, August 8, 1945.
16. Material provided by Hampton University.
17. Henry G. Badger, U.S. Office of Education, "Effect of the War on Negro Education," 1944 Proceedings, p. 29.
18. 1945 Proceedings, p. 41.
19. Durrell A. Hiller, Vocational Rehabilitation and Education Division, Veterans Administration, New Orleans, LA, 1945 Proceedings, p. 51.
20. Ibid., p. 55.
21. W.J. Trent, Jr., United Negro College Fund, "The United Negro College Fund," 1944 Proceedings, p. 41.
22. V.D. Johnston, Howard University, "Some Problems Immediately Ahead of the Business Officer," 1941 Proceedings, p. 44.
23. Leon A. Ransom, Howard University, "A Review of the Application of the Gaines Decision," 1944 Proceedings, p. 48.
24. Ibid., p. 50.
25. Ibid., p. 51.

26. Ibid., p. 55.

27. Nelson H. Harris, Shaw University, "The Present Status of Higher Education among Negroes in North Carolina," 1942 Proceedings, pp. 37-38.

28. Ibid., p. 38.

29. Ibid.

30. Charles L. Franklin, Social Security Board, Washington, DC, "Present Status of Social Security Legislation Affecting Institutions of Higher Education," 1942 Proceedings, p. 70.

31. Louis H. Schuster, Virginia State College, "The Virginia Retirement System," 1942 Proceedings, p. 82.

32. Robert O. Purves, Hampton Institute, "Student Labor As Applied to Construction Work at Hampton Institute," 1939 Proceedings, pp. 27-28.

33. 1944 Proceedings, p. 18.

34. Ibid., p. 19.

35. Executive Committee minutes, 1945 Proceedings, p. 84.

4

New Challenges to Higher Education: 1946-1949

The period between the last year of World War II and the beginning of the next decade presented serious challenges to administrators in higher education. Chief among these were the adaptations required for dealing with an influx of returning veterans, a widespread scarcity of housing, and other problems of moving from a wartime to a peacetime economy.

Topics of Interest at Meetings in the Postwar Years

Returning Veterans

Four separate papers at the 1946 meeting dealt with the issue of returning veterans, and the topic was presented again in 1947. The difficulties to be encountered in handling financial arrangements for the education of veterans, under legislation allowing government benefits for this purpose, were discussed in two papers, one in each year. (The complexity of the regulations covering payments to educational institutions for the training and education of veterans must have increased the business officer's usual headaches tenfold.)

Two other 1946 addresses, on an advisory service and on guidance for veterans, described the need to assist veterans in making correct training and job decisions. A fifth paper in 1946, addressing the problem of housing for veterans, was given by Albert L. Thompson, racial relations advisor, Region IV, Federal Public Housing Authority, Atlanta. Thompson commented that "we are suffering not only from a critical lack of good homes but from a shortage of shelter of any kind."[1] He stated that reasons for the shortage included an inadequate supply of good homes even before the war, lack of home maintenance during the war because materials were needed elsewhere, and finally the demobilization of the armed forces after the war. The remainder of the paper discussed the use of temporary public housing for servicemen, which was under the auspices of the newly created Federal Public Housing Authority. Institutions of higher education were closely involved with this problem, of course, because so many veterans returning to school were married and required housing for families.

Physical Plant

Papers addressing issues connected with physical plant appeared on the programs of meetings in 1946, 1947, and 1949. (Veterans' housing problems, mentioned above, can be included in this category.) Those papers pointed up a recurring problem on college campuses—lack of funding for proper maintenance of plant. The problem was made worse in the late forties by the lack of materials and skilled labor and the pressing need for new and expanded facilities.

Endowments and Other Topics

Endowments were the topic of two presentations in those years, as business officers sought advice on means of supporting a growing enrollment and new program demands. Also, sources of funds available to independent black institutions were changing and there was a need to seek endowments.

A brief return on the part of the American Association to addresses on black higher education—chiefly in state institutions—occurred in the meetings of 1947 and 1948: in 1947, "Financial History of Higher Education for Negroes in Texas," was presented by A. Maceo Smith, president, Texas Negro Chamber of Commerce, and "State Appropriations for Institutions of Higher Learning in Texas," by T.R. Solomon, registrar and coordinator of institutions, Prairie View Agricultural and Mechanical College; and in 1948, "The Financial History of Higher Education for Negroes in Florida," was given by A.S. Parks, professor of history, Florida A&M College, and "The Outlook for Higher Education among Negroes in Florida," by William H. Gray, Jr., president, Florida A&M College.

A variety of topics of traditional interest to business officers occupied most of the space on the programs of the meetings from 1946 through 1949, including internal reports, personnel administration, the relationship between the business officer and the board of directors and between the business officer and the faculty, procurement, accounting techniques, public relations, insurance, and athletics. The papers reflected the maturing of the American Association and indicated that black institutions were finding it possible, slowly, to enter more fully into the mainstream of American life. Though none of these changes were as dramatic as those of the fifties and sixties, there was a sense that black administrators were quietly moving into their rightful place in America's social structure.

Professional Development

Several talks at Association meetings from 1946-1949 presented various aspects of professional development for business officers, such as "Business Officers in Spheres of Influence," by Robert Daniel, president, Shaw University, in 1946, and an address by E.C. McLeod, president, Wiley College, in 1947. Both papers showed the respect that chief executive officers had for business and financial administrators, demonstrating the advances made by business officers since the early days of higher education.

Perhaps the most important talk on professional development was given by V.D. Johnston in 1948, in response to a suggestion at the previous American Association meeting that some thought should be given to the words of the Association's "Purpose" (see p. 26). Titled "Professional Standards for the Business Officer," Johnston's brief paper offered a thoughtful, thorough set of standards that are as fresh and generally applicable at this writing as when they were first formulated. They deserve to be quoted in their entirety:

> 1. *Training.* The first test of the professional competence of the business officer is his ability to train himself for his position. This training is pointed in three directions. The first is to acquire ability in the use of the mechanical devices, such as bookkeeping, budgets, and records, as they relate to education. The second is to inform himself on the organization, aims, purposes, policies, and needs of the institution he serves. The third is to secure general training. The first type of training can be undertaken more deliberately than the second; neither can ever be regarded as finally accomplished. Contact with others is a chief requisite for development in either area. The business officer will have to seek constantly for books and magazines that relate to his work. Publications of the five as-

sociations of business officers have substantial information for this purpose. Membership in one or more and attendance at one or more of the annual meetings is a necessity for professional development of any business officer.

2. *Conduct*. Conduct involves relationships and thoughtful action. The typical educational institution has a governing board, a president as chief executive officer responsible to the board, a dean responsible to the president in academic matters, and a business officer responsible to the president in business matters. Almost without exception, academic policies have business implications, and business procedures have to be shaped to academic policy. In relations with students the business officer is involved in their first mature conception of a businessman. Professional conduct is involved in the application of the business officer's understanding, responsibility, and authority to daily action. The business officer has the duty to maintain the records and provide the information required by the governing board . . . and as required by the president. In any matter related to his particular office, he has the responsibility to put before the president, and to urge upon the president, if necessary, such policies as concern the business office. Action thereafter, if any, is a responsibility of the chief executive officer.

Professional conduct of the business officer has broader influence than this. Because so many academic policies have business implications, not always considered by persons with academic responsibilities, the business officer must be constantly aware of what is being proposed from every quarter and formulate in his own mind a considered opinion on each such proposal. Professional conduct requires that the opinion be withheld until asked for by the chief executive officer. The business officer should concern himself with the formulation of academic policies only to the extent of their financial implications.

3. *Employment*. The business officer is employed by the governing board on recommendation of the chief executive officer. Professional standards involve term of employment, status, and salary.

Each of these considerations is relative to standards existing within the institution. Since institutions exist in a competitive situation, each has to be considered in relation to a best standard, to what obtains in the "best" institutions.

Term of employment in the educational institution has significance for the business officer as it does for the teacher. If it is a policy of the institution to employ the president or the dean with indefinite tenure, the same policy should apply to the business officer. An initial or trial appointment may be made for a short term. Applied to a best standard, reason is on the side of indefinite tenure for a business officer who has proven satisfactory after initial appointment for a stated term. When policies have to be discussed, the business officer who has to face an annual vote of confidence may feel constrained to reflect only the opinion of the one who makes the recommendation for his reappointment. The atmosphere and opportunity for frank discussions and honest disagreement are necessary to secure support for established policy.

Status, in the employment of the business officer, involves relationships with others within and without the institution. The business officer, to use familiar terms, is a staff officer to the extent that he is called upon to consider and report upon policies and finances of the institution as a whole; he is a line officer to the extent that he is directly responsible for the record keeping, budget, buildings and grounds, auxiliary enterprises and the like. This is so even if he has under his supervision others with direct responsibility to him for these separate functions. Strength in organization, best practice, and the existing practice in the great majority of institutions require the grouping of these functions under one business officer. Whenever contrary practice exists, it requires explanation.

Status for the business officer is imposed to the extent that his opinion is sought in a staff capacity. Status is earned to the extent that he fulfills his responsibility as a line officer. Professional conduct is involved in each capacity. As a staff officer he has responsibility to know what is happening about him and to formulate a consid-

Don A. Davis   Virginius D. Johnston

J.R.E. Lee, Jr.   Luther H. Foster, Sr.

Delegates at the first, or organizational, meeting of the Association of Business Officers in Schools for Negroes, Howard University, Washington, DC, April 13-15, 1939.

Delegates at the twenty-eighth and final meeting of the American Association of College and University Business Officers, North Carolina College, Durham, North Carolina, May 11-13, 1967.

Officers of the Association of Business Officers in Schools for Negroes, 1942.

A.L. Palmer, Howard University, in Pilot Training Program at Tuskegee Institute, Alabama; graduated 2nd Lieutenant, August 1945.

A workshop session at an annual meeting of the American Association of College and University Business Officers, early 1960s.

NACUBO Board of Directors, 1965, including American Association representatives Burnett A. Little, A.L. Palmer, and James W. Bryant.

ered opinion. This can be stated only when called for, with a mind detached, and he must be prepared to support a decision by the chief executive quite to the contrary. As a line officer he has responsibility to act directly in several related functions: records, budget, finances, buildings and grounds, and auxiliary enterprises. Status is earned to the extent that he advances the welfare of the institution as a whole in these related functions. In this capacity there is not the requirement for reticence and detachment in the statement of facts or formulated opinion. Status, in this sense, is based upon confidence, and confidence rests upon a knowledge of the facts. As an example, it is not sufficient for the financial report to go to the president and the governing board, and be included in the printed report, perhaps in abbreviated form, for all state educational institutions. There is a larger constituency to be fully informed, within and without the institution, if confidence, based on the facts, is to exist on the subject of the institution's finances. Such a published report should have a certificate to indicate independent audit of the records. There are probably very few business officers now who are not independently bonded, at the expense of the institution.

Salary of the business officer should not be based upon acceptance of perquisites and no perquisites should be granted by the institution that are not common to any other employed member of the institution. Salary should be sufficient to preclude any justification for employment of relatives of the business officer in the same institution.

Since there is usually only one chief business officer in each institution, the question of salary is often one of benevolent consideration, or periodic individual bargaining. Either method is a violation of professional conduct, and a more objective method should be found. Since salaries are related within the institution, and influenced by competitive factors outside, it is suggested that the salary of the business officer should never be less than two-thirds that of the chief executive, including perquisites. This rule of thumb can be checked by (a) comparison of salaries in similar institutions, taking varying cost-of-living factors into account, (b) appraisal by independent agency, as, for instance, a state or other classification board, or (c) inquiry as to payment for similar responsibility in industry.[2]

President's Commission

An address at the 1948 meeting that carried implications for the future of black educators and administrators was the "Report on the President's Commission on Higher Education," by John Dale Russell, director of the Division of Higher Education, U.S. Office of Education. In his talk Russell pointed out that the commission, which had been appointed by President Truman in 1946, was to consider problems specifically relevant to higher education, rather than studying education in general as several previous presidential commissions had done.

The resulting report, completed in December 1947, was published in six volumes and covered such topics as "Equalizing and Expanding Individual Opportunity," "Staffing Higher Education," and "Financing Higher Education."[3] Russell briefly discussed questions raised by the report, such as the following: Who should receive higher education? What barriers exist to higher education? Do we need so many educated people? Russell spoke on both economic barriers (and what might be done to remove them) and discrimination:

> The second barrier, to which extensive treatment is given, is discrimination in admissions. Racial discrimination is discussed [in the report] primarily with respect to the plight of the Negro student. After a careful review of the available data, a majority of the "Commission concludes that there will be no fundamental correction of the total condition until segregation legislation is repealed."[4]

Seventh Meeting—1946

The seventh annual meeting of the Association took place on May 9-11, 1946, at Shaw University in Raleigh, North Carolina.

In his opening remarks, the president of the Association, G. Leon Netterville of Southern University, stressed the Association's appreciation to Shaw for providing accommodation, since "it seemed for awhile as if our Association would be unable to hold its meeting, due to the acute housing situation on most of the campuses of our members."[5] The fact that American Association members were still obliged to meet on member campuses, rather than in local hotels, further exacerbated the situation.

Eighth Meeting—1947

The 1947 meeting of the American Association was hosted jointly in Marshall, Texas, by Bishop and Wiley Colleges. The Monday program was held at Wiley, the Tuesday program at Bishop.

Two resolutions presented by the Resolutions Committee stated prevailing interests of the time:

> Inasmuch as there appear to be confusion and uncertainty in the minds of many of our members as to the best procedure to follow in procuring educational and maintenance equipment and material from federal agencies, thereby affecting savings to our institutions amounting to thousands of dollars;

> Be it resolved: That the president and the secretary be here requested to gather all information possible in forms of releases, circulars and directives and forward the same to the respective members.

> Be it further resolved: That resolutions of encouragement and approval be sent to those responsible for drafting and presenting the numerous bills now being considered in Congress or about to be offered for consideration, which if enacted will greatly benefit the cause of education generally and the education of the Negro specifically.[6]

It was voted at the meeting that the president of the American Association should appoint a committee to study the Association's statement of purpose, and bring to the next meeting some comments on the implications. (See p. 49 for V.D. Johnston's paper resulting from that study.)

Ninth Meeting—1948

Florida A&M College, Tallahassee, Florida, was chosen as the site for the 1948 meeting. The college was founded by the Florida state legislature in 1887 as a state normal school, on what later became the site of Florida State University. The college was moved to its second home, on "another of the seven hills of Tallahassee,"[7] in 1891. In 1905 it was placed under the state Board of Control as one of Florida's institutions of higher learning.

The Resolutions Committee offered two resolutions that, as in the previous year, took note of events of particular interest to Association members:

In view of recent trends in the field of higher education with respect to the establishment of regional institutions of higher learning, and as it is apparent that these trends are for the sole purpose of perpetuating the undemocratic principle of racial segregation in the field of higher education;

Be it resolved: That the Association of Business Officers in Schools for Negroes express its opposition to the establishment of such schools and instruct its president to convey this expression to any and all agencies who are actively opposing legislation in the National Congress and individual states that would make the establishment of such schools possible.

A number of business institutions are now offering employment to trained Negroes and financial aid to qualified Negro students, all of which lends itself to raising the economic and educational level of our group;

Be it therefore resolved: That members of the Association be urged to cooperate with these business institutions whenever and wherever possible.[8]

The Committee on Time and Place suggested that the Pershing Hotel in Chicago be considered as a site for the 1949 American Association meeting, to mark the occasion of the Association's tenth anniversary. As it happened, the tenth meeting was actually held in Atlanta, Georgia.

The last item of business for the 1948 meeting was a vote of thanks to V.D. Johnston for his "efforts to secure fuller integration of membership in the several associations of business officers."[9]

Tenth Anniversary Meeting—1949

Five institutions in Atlanta, Georgia, acted together to host the American Association's tenth anniversary meeting: Atlanta University, Clark College, Morehouse College, Morris Brown College, and Spelman College.

The first resolution presented by the Committee on Resolutions reiterated the vote of thanks offered to V.D. Johnston in the preceding meeting, but stated this in expanded form:

Whereas Mr. V. D. Johnston, quiet and unassuming gentleman, humble and self-effacing to a fault, conceived the

idea and fostered the organization and growth of the Association of Business Officers in Schools for Negroes, and

Whereas the services he has rendered this Association
have been invaluable and beyond accurate appraisal, and

Whereas this organization feels the need for his continued
counsel and assistance as it charts its course for the future,

Be it therefore resolved: That the Association of Business
Officers in Schools for Negroes herewith take cognizance
of the service of a great personality and accord him a vote
of thanks and that the organization go on record as encouraging his continued interest in and support of the
Association of Business Officers in Schools for Negroes.[10]

The reason for the extended vote of thanks soon became apparent—
Johnston was leaving higher education. It was suggested that both
he and Luther H. Foster, Sr., be made honorary members of the
Association. A sad note that year was the death of Lloyd Isaacs,
treasurer of Tuskegee Institute. He had helped organize the American
Association and had recently served on its Executive Committee.

Other items of note at the tenth meeting included suggestions
that a committee be appointed to consider a name change for the
Association and that "no commercial representatives be scheduled
on the official program of the Association, but arrangements be
permitted for exhibits, if this is possible in the space available, through
the host institution."[11]

A new name was, indeed, adopted at the eleventh meeting in 1950,
which was the beginning of a new decade and a time of events that
would have far-reaching effects on predominantly black institutions
of higher education.

References—Chapter 4

1. Albert L. Thompson, Federal Public Housing Authority, Atlanta,
   Georgia, 1946 Proceedings, p. 59.
2. V.D. Johnston, Howard University, "Professional Standards for the
   Business Officer," 1948 Proceedings, pp. 35-37.
3. John Dale Russell, U.S. Office of Education, "The Report of the
   President's Commission on Higher Education," 1948 Proceedings,
   p. 13.
4. Ibid., p. 17.

5. G. Leon Netterville, Southern University, opening remarks, 1946 Proceedings, p. 13.

6. 1947 Proceedings, pp. 88-89.

7. A.S. Parks, Florida A&M College, "The Financial History of Higher Education for Negroes in Florida," 1948 Proceedings, p. 30.

8. 1948 Proceedings, p. 78.

9. Ibid., p. 79.

10. 1949 Proceedings, p. 47.

11. Ibid., p. 50.

5

Evolution and Revolution: 1950-1959

Evolutionary changes affected the work of college and university business officers in the 1950s, both externally and internally: for example, institutions were becoming more and more involved with federal government aid and its ramifications, which closely involved business officers. Of importance to the internal workings of the industry were such issues as the rise of a national federation of business officers and the writing of a new manual on college and university business administration—the first such volume to be produced as the result of consensus of practitioners throughout the industry.

Higher education was also radically affected by various forces during the fifties: the country became embroiled in a war in Korea in 1950-1953, only five years after the end of World War II, and, perhaps most important for the members of the American Association, a series of laws and court decisions mandated the first significant movement toward integration of the races in many phases of American life.

The 1950 Proceedings were the first to carry two names on the title page: the old Association name, under which it had been founded, and a new name, voted on at that meeting—the "American Association of College Business Officers." The old name was changed because it tended, automatically, to "restrict the membership" and did not reflect "the democratic spirit which should prevail in . . . organizations of this type."[1] The group was to be known by the new name until 1961, when the words "and University" were added before "Business Officers," to express more correctly the growth experienced by its members.[2]

Topics Presented at Meetings during the 1950s

Legislative Developments

"Current Legislative Developments of Significance to Higher Education" was the theme of addresses presented at meetings in 1950, 1951, and 1952. The 1950 presentation, by George N. Redd, professor of education, Fisk University, began with a recapitulation of the report of the President's Commission on Higher Education (1947) and went on to discuss the "more than two hundred bills dealing with education in some form" then pending in Congress.[3] Two of those proposals stand out, in the light of hindsight: a bill to set up an independent agency to be known as the National Science Foundation, "whose purpose would be to encourage, initiate, and support scientific research"; and a movement to establish a "federal program of scholarships and fellowships to enable capable young people to continue their education beyond the secondary level."[4] Of interest, too, in Redd's presentation was a section on "Southern Regional Education," which briefly described an attempt to establish cooperative regional programs for higher education—a move that was regarded with "distrust and suspicion in certain circles" because of the fear that it would help to perpetuate segregated education in the South.[5]

In 1951 Preston C. Johnson, professor of education, Virginia State College, approached the topic of legislative developments from the standpoint of various court decisions. He first discussed a joint resolution of the Kentucky senate that said the state:

> . . . shall not erect, acquire, develop or maintain in any manner any educational institution within its borders to which Negroes shall not be admitted on an equal basis with other races nor shall any Negro citizen of Kentucky be forced to attend any segregated regional institution to obtain instruction in a particular course of study if there is in operation within the Commonwealth at the time an institution that offers the same course of study to students of other races.[6]

In his conclusion Johnson offered three suggestions regarding the "war on discrimination": (1) that the "proof of unfair and discriminatory allocation of public funds should be proof of nonfeasance as well as misfeasance in public office," (2) that an administrative agency that delays the grant of a right [in this case a constitutional guarantee] is guilty of denying the right and should be answerable in civil action for damages to any petitioner who could show proof of such delay, and (3) that a continuous assault should be maintained on the "separate but equal" doctrine.[7]

Walter G. Daniel, specialist for higher education in the Office of Education, Washington, DC, addressed current legislative developments in 1952. He indicated that, according to one estimate, as many as 1,000 bills relating to education had been presented during the Eighty-First Congress. Daniel mentioned legislation on financial assistance for veterans' education, for students generally, and for institutions; universal military training; tax assessment and exemption; and the elimination of segregation and discrimination. Under the last, Daniel discussed H.R. 5945, introduced by Rep. Jacob Javits (R-NY). That bill sought to have Congress declare:

> . . . that it is its purpose to strengthen and secure the civil rights of the people of the United States under the Constitution, and that it is the national policy to protect the right of the individual to be free from discrimination or segregation based upon race, color, religion, or national origin.
>
> [Daniel added that:] Various sections of the bill deal with lynching, discrimination in employment, segregation in housing, protection of civil rights, and education. Title V says that it shall be an unfair practice for an educational institution to "exclude, limit, or otherwise discriminate against any person or persons seeking admission as students to such institutions because of race, religion, color, or national origin."[8]

Professional Development

Professional development, in various aspects, is a recurring theme throughout the fifties in American Association programs. Treatment of this topic included a talk at the 1951 meeting dealing with the individual business officer as exemplar of his position, and a thoughtful, scholarly paper by Don A. Davis, "The Profession of College Business Management," at the 1953 meeting. A presentation in 1956 addressed the fiduciary responsibility of business officers, a talk in 1957 dealt with the business manager and his preparation for the coming decade of the sixties, and a 1959 address discussed the need for recognition of the professionalism required of business officers.

Financing Higher Education

The problems of financing higher education were discussed several times at meetings during the 1950s, in terms of student tuition and fees, fund raising, government aid, investments, and other areas.

Other Topics

A wide range of other topics was covered at meetings from 1950 to 1959, including those with which business officers are involved every day: purchasing, insurance, retirement and social security, records management, budgeting, costs of operations, auxiliary enterprises, and physical plant. Concerning the last-named, a presentation on "The College Housing Loan Program," by George C. Decker, chief of the program, was given at the 1952 meeting. This address reflected the urgent needs of colleges and universities across the country for more housing to accommodate the tide of students that had been rising since the end of World War II. Korean War veterans were beginning to join the ranks and there was a universal need for government loan assistance to deal with the problem.

Auditing, internal control, and personnel received more emphasis on programs at meetings during the fifties than ever before. And among the topics presented were several that were completely new: institutional research, modern data processing, use of space, and "The Administration Education Proposals," presented in 1958 by Lloyd E. Blauch, assistant commissioner for higher education, U.S. Office of Education (then part of the Department of Health, Education and Welfare). Blauch's presentation reflected the alarm that had been raised in the United States over the launching by the U.S.S.R. of "Sputnik," the world's first spacecraft, in October 1957. "The great problem here," said Blauch, "is to salvage all the brainpower of the nation. . . . We have become very much alarmed . . . because we see the great progress that the Russians are making in developing their skilled manpower. We are waking up to the fact that we have to make the most of [our manpower] or in the long run we shall be left behind in the race which is going on in the world today."[9]

A follow-on to the preceding address was a presentation on the National Defense Education Act, given at the 1959 meeting by Byron Donegas, of the U.S. Office of Education. The address described the act and the eight titles that came under the province of the Office of Education. They were listed as follows:

Title II—Loans to Students

Title III—Strengthening Instruction in Elementary and Secondary Schools

Title IV—Fellowships for Graduate Students

Title V—Testing and Counseling Institutes and State Programs

Title VI—Foreign Language Training Centers and Institutes

Title VII—Improvement of Educational Utilization of Television, Radio, Motion Pictures, and Related Media of Communication

Title VIII—Providing Area Vocational Education Facilities

Title X—Improving Statistical Services [10]

New subjects at the 1950 meeting included student accounts and accreditation. An address on financial support for higher education for blacks in Georgia was given in 1953 by L.R. Bywaters, comptroller of Fort Valley State College. And—interesting for the opposite picture that it presented—a paper titled "The Public Negro College in a Racially Integrated System of Higher Education" was presented in 1952 by R.B. Atwood, president of Kentucky State College. Atwood spoke of the impact of racial integration on black institutions in Kentucky and looked ahead to what full integration might ultimately mean for black institutions throughout the South.

National Federation

An event of significance to business officers throughout the country, but especially to those affiliated with one of the four regional associations and the American Association, was the formation in 1950 of a National Federation of College and University Business Officers Associations. In addition to the American Association and the four regionals, the National Association of Educational Buyers also had membership in the Federation. [11] Luther H. Foster, Jr., was the American Association's first representative to the Federation, which would eventually be replaced by the National Association of College and University Business Officers (NACUBO).

In the minutes of the 1952 Proceedings of the American Association, a review of a Federation meeting was mentioned. A resolution for that meeting promised continued support for the Federation, which was to cost each member institution two dollars. In addition, an appendix was attached to the minutes: a report to members of the Federation from the Federation president, Jamie R. Anthony of the Georgia Institute of Technology. In the report are listed the Federation's "future objectives":

1. To provide through representation of the herein listed Associations in the National Federation, means whereby agencies of the federal government may ascertain opinions and points of view on all matters involving fiscal and business matters of national interest to colleges and universities.

2. To initiate, formulate and represent to government agencies matters of common business interest to colleges and universities.

3. To give nationwide interest and scope to the work of developing and improving principles and practices of education and business administration.

4. To collect and disseminate among the membership of the various associations listed herein new and useful information.

5. To refer changes or additions to these objectives for ratification to the member Associations through their respective executive committees.[12]

Mentioned in Anthony's report was the work of an interassociation committee that had existed since 1948 (in 1954 it became a committee of the Federation) to represent universities in contacts with the Department of Defense, the Veterans Administration, the Public Health Service, and the Atomic Energy Commission. The American Association member on this committee, which was chaired by William T. Middlebrook of the University of Minnesota, was James B. Clarke, then treasurer of Howard University.[13]

A further report on activities of the National Federation was given at the 1953 meeting, and in 1954 Clarke delivered "A Report on the National Federation of Business Officers Associations Study of Income and Expenditure Classification"—the so-called "Sixty-College Study." Twelve members of the American Association participated in the study, whose purpose was to provide comparative data for use in dealing with financial and administrative problems in small colleges. The 12 American Association participants were: Bennett College, Spelman College, Morehouse College, Lincoln University

(Pennsylvania), Bethune Cookman College, Clark College, Dillard University, Fisk University, Talladega College, Shaw University, Texas College, and North Carolina College at Durham. In 1955 Clarke gave a progress report on the National Federation study project and commented on accounting information gathered in Volume I of *College & University Business Administration.*

In the minutes of the 1955 Proceedings, the secretary's report included the following statement: "Your Secretary served as one of the Association's three representatives on the Board of Directors of the National Federation."[14] The secretary at the time was Burnett A. Little. The report also commented on the involvement of the Federation in the "Sixty-College Study." A brief report attached to the minutes of the 1956 Proceedings, given by James W. Bryant, business manager of Texas College, mentioned the first National Assembly of the Federation, held in Estes Park, Colorado, in June 1955. Bryant lists Harold K. Logan, Charles E. Prothro, Jr. (resident auditor of Tuskegee Institute), J.R.E. Lee, Jr., and Isaiah T. Creswell (comptroller of Fisk University) as representatives at the Assembly from the American Association. James B. Clarke gave a separate report, also at the 1956 meeting, on the "Sixty-College Study."

The Proceedings for 1958 listed that year's American Association representatives to the National Federation: Wendell G. Morgan, assistant treasurer, Howard University; Sinclair V. Jeter, business manager, Clark College; and William M. Jones, business manager, North Carolina College. The Association resolutions for that year reflected activities of the Federation, in that the Association "approves in principle the plan for a permanent full-time Secretary of the National Federation of College and University Business Officers Associations; however, the Association reserves such approval pending the determination of any and all increased cost to the Association relative thereto and the presented function of the office."[15] Another resolution agreed to increase the "dues per member institution to the National Federation of College and University Business Officers Associations from $2.00 to $4.00 per year."[16]

CUBA: Volumes I and II

Work on a manual on college and university business administration was first discussed in the minutes of the 1950 meeting, where mention was made of a "Committee on Publication of a College Business Manual."[17] Luther H. Foster, Jr., reported on activities of the committee, which was working to produce a document that would cover all aspects of business and financial administration in colleges and universities, and would benefit from the expertise of many business officers. Foster represented the American Association on the "National Committee on the Preparation of a Manual on College and University Business Administration" (its official title), which had begun work as early as 1942 with funds from grants made to the American Council on Education. The four regional associations of business officers and the American Association also contributed to the funds.[18] Volume I of the manual was published in 1952 and Volume II in 1955.[19]

Harold K. Logan, then business manager at Tuskegee Institute, presented at the 1955 meeting a "Review of *College & University Business Administration*, Volume II." He described the methods used to obtain consensus on the information presented in both volumes, and stated that "James B. Clarke, treasurer of Howard University, and Luther H. Foster, Jr., [who had become] president of Tuskegee Institute, represented the American Association on the National Committee" for preparing the book.[20] He ended with a detailed description of the chapters contained in Volume II. Financial assistance in the preparation of Volumes I and II was provided by the member associations of the National Federation; the American Association gave $200.[21] In the minutes of the 1953 Proceedings, it was reported that the General Education Board had made a grant of $30,000 to assist with the publication of Volume II.[22]

Training and Internship

The training of candidates to become college or university business officers—initiated informally long before the formation of the American Association—was to remain a major interest of the group throughout its existence.

At the 1955 Association meeting, Charles E. Prothro, Jr., Tuskegee Institute, reported on an "Intern Training Program for College Business Officers," of which he was the coordinator. Begun the previous September, the training program was a formalized continuation of pioneer efforts in the area. Prothro described the program as follows:

> Twelve months of intensive work experience in the several business areas of the Institute constitute the core of the program. This includes assignments in plant maintenance, construction management, accounting, cashiering, purchasing management, organization and administration, cafeteria operation, hospital services, and

management of other auxiliary enterprises. In addition, the training experience is enriched by special lectures, seminars, and field trips to other institutions. A bibliography has been prepared. The intern is expected to do extensive reading and to make book reviews. He is also required to take two formal courses in the field of education during his tenure at the Institute.[23]

The above was listed as part of the program of the meeting, and a brief report on the internship program appeared in the minutes of each succeeding meeting in the 1950s. The training program had mixed success; in some years many candidates applied, while in others only a few. At least 20 persons went through the program, which continued from 1954 to 1963.[24]

Placement Service

The 1950 meeting saw the first of a series of reports by the Association's placement officer. The reports varied in length and detail, but their prominence in the committee records indicated the importance that Association members attached to the placement service. In the 1950s it was still a major means by which black administrators found jobs and predominantly black institutions filled positions.

Newsletter

Beginning in 1950 the American Association voted to extend its newsletter as the "official organ" of the Association.[25] From that time onward, the newsletter was frequently mentioned in the minutes of Association meetings. It was used as a vehicle for distributing (1) information to members about activities on their campuses, such as new building construction or personnel changes relevant to the business officer function, and (2) important information from other sources, such as how to obtain surplus supplies at special rates or where to get help in interpreting or carrying out certain government regulations. The newsletter also solicited information from its members and served as an advance notice for the annual American Association meeting.

Shift in Association Emphasis

A gradual shift in emphasis in the activities and concerns of the American Association in the 1950s was evidenced in the Proceedings and other documents of the decade. At the beginning of the Association's existence, long and varied annual meeting programs, featuring heavily substantive addresses that offered much basic information, had been the norm. As the Association matured, however, the meeting programs concentrated more on several specific topics each time.

The energies of the Association members and officers turned more toward activities such as the National Federation, involvement with U.S. government agencies, and professional interaction among themselves. This change represented not only the growing sophistication of the Association, but also the slowly accelerating assimilation of black educators and administrators into the main currents of American life. In this history, the Association's shift of emphasis is apparent in the decreasing reportage on topics addressed at meetings and the increasing amount of information on member activities outside annual meetings.

Eleventh Meeting—1950

Fisk University and Tennessee A&I State College, both of Nashville, TN, served as hosts for the eleventh meeting of the American Association.

Fisk University opened as Fisk School in January 1866, under the auspices of the American Missionary Association of New York City (later a part of the United Church of Christ) and the Western Freedmen's Aid Commission of Cincinnati. The institution was named for General Clinton B. Fisk of the Freedmen's Bureau in Tennessee.

Fisk University passed through successive stages of grade school, secondary school, and normal school on its way to becoming a university. Although basically concerned with the needs of black students, its charter stated that the school's purpose was the "education and training of young men and women, irrespective of color."[26]

An important "sign of the times," the increased involvement of the federal government with institutional affairs, was reflected in the report by James B. Clarke on the activities of the interassociation committee, which then was concerned primarily with scientific research contracts. The group was also discussing "taxes on real estate and lease-back arrangements which are under criticism by the Federal Government."[27] The Association voted to retain Clarke as its representative in the Washington area.

Progress in the area of integration can be seen in Clarke's comments, in which he urged Association members to attend more sessions of the Eastern and Central Associations (EACUBO and CA-CUBO). Finally, it was noted that several members had died during the year, including Luther H. Foster, Sr., one of the Association's founders, who had gone on to become president of Virginia State College after years of service in business administration at that institution.

Twelfth Meeting—1951

The 1951 American Association meeting took place at Virginia State College, Petersburg, Virginia, on May 6-8. The college, now known as Virginia State University, was founded in 1882 as the Virginia Normal and Collegiate Institute and was the first fully state-supported black college in America. Later, the college acquired a branch at Norfolk. The curriculum initially provided for preparatory courses, normal teacher training, and collegiate studies, and eventually expanded to 40 undergraduate offerings and 26 graduate degree programs. The institution led its state in desegregation when it appointed its first full-time white faculty member in 1964.[28]

Of note at this meeting was a change in dues: at the previous meeting, they were still $10 per institution, but according to member information in the 1951 Proceedings, they became $20 that year. Items discussed at the meeting included plans for possible regional workshops and for using the Association newsletter to obtain suggestions for the next meeting program. It was mentioned that college buildings and grounds officers were considering the formation of an association of their own.

Thirteenth Meeting—1952

The thirteenth meeting of the American Association was held at Kentucky State College, Frankfort, Kentucky, on May 4-6, 1952.

Among the items of business reported in the minutes of that meeting was the need for an assistant secretary to help the Association secretary in his duties, especially those relating to the annual meeting. This matter was referred to the Executive Committee.

Fourteenth Meeting—1953

Fort Valley State College, Fort Valley, Georgia, hosted the fourteenth annual meeting on May 3-5, 1953. The president's report for that year stated that he and the Association secretary had represented the Association at the third annual meeting of the National Federation in Chicago the previous summer. He further stated that Luther H. Foster, Jr. (Association secretary) had been named to the Federation Nominating Committee and that he, J.R.E. Lee, Jr., had been named to the Federation's Resolutions Committee. Lee commented that 63 out of a potential 92 institutions were members of the American Association, and urged members to take a more active part in recruiting.

A report by Foster, Jr., also mentioned membership, describing campaigns that had been conducted both to enroll new members and to reinstate delinquent members. In addition, he commented on the newsletter and gave brief reports on the National Federation and on the progress of Volume II of *College & University Business Administration*.

Of interest in the minutes for this meeting were the number of invitations extended to the American Association to send representatives to various other meetings, including those held by the National Association of Educational Buyers and the College and University Personnel Association. It was evident that the American Association was, by then, well past its formative years and had been accepted as "establishment" among its colleague associations. The secretary's report further commented on his membership on the editorial board of *College and University Business* magazine (the magazine merged with *Nations' Schools* in September 1974).[29]

It was reported that the buildings and grounds personnel had not been able to project enough interest to form their own organization, and that they thus wished to continue meeting with the American Association.

Fifteenth Meeting—1954

The Association met at Lincoln University, Jefferson City, Missouri, on May 2-4, 1954. The president reported that year that the Association secretary, Luther H. Foster, Jr., had been promoted to president of Tuskegee Institute, and a new secretary had been appointed: Burnett A. "Burnie" Little, of Southern University in Baton Rouge.

Also featured in the president's report was the college business management institute in Omaha, with the comment that "it is gratifying to note that one-tenth of the total enrollment . . . consisted of students identified with this Association."[30] Association members were also urged to participate in the summer institute at the University of Kentucky.

In the secretary's report it was noted that a questionnaire had been sent out to Association members to obtain their comments about initiating among member institutions a training program for college business officers. Don A. Davis of Hampton Institute spoke at length on the subject at the annual meeting.

Sixteenth Meeting—1955

Arkansas AM&N College, Pine Bluff, Arkansas, acted as host to the 1955 meeting, held on May 1-3. Of special import to Association members that year were the last paragraphs of the report by the president of the Association, W.C. Ervin of Arkansas AM&N:

> It is almost impossible . . . to address an audience of educated men and women and not mention the historic proclamation of the U.S. Supreme Court eleven months ago, that separate educational facilities are inherently unequal and that segregation is unconstitutional.
>
> The Supreme Court is expected to give its decision before the end of June as to how and when [desegregation will take place]. None of us present know what the decision will be; but one thing all of us agree on: segregation in any form is cruel, mean, it is undemocratic and it is unchristian. Those of us in this country who are wise will be tolerant of each other, yet we will work together, not sacrificing any principle to bring about full integration in the schools, thus confirming the fact that all men are created equal and that 16,000,000 Negroes deserve their rights as first-class American citizens.[31]

Seventeenth Meeting—1956

The American Association met April 29 to May 1, 1956, at Winston-Salem Teachers College, Winston-Salem, North Carolina. The minutes of the seventeenth meeting included a report from James B. Clarke on scholarships offered by the Carnegie Foundation to send certain persons to the week-long summer college business management institute in Omaha. In the report of the Resolutions Committee, thanks were extended to all the member colleges that participated in the "Sixty-College Study" and to those that took part in a study conducted by the United Negro College Fund.

Eighteenth Meeting—1957

On May 2-4, 1957, Hampton Institute was host for a second time to an American Association meeting. Included in the president's report was a comment on the active participation of American Association members in meetings of the Central and Eastern Associations. Harold K. Logan, that year's president, also noted his own participation in deliberations of the President's Committee on Education beyond the High School. Logan strongly urged Association members to support all available sources of professional development, such as by attending the summer business management institutes and helping to sustain the internship training program at Tuskegee Institute.

A report from the secretary stated that the Executive Committee had determined that the three official representatives of the American Association to the National Federation should be the president, secretary, and immediate past president of the Association. The Association allowed $50 toward each representative's expenses, with the rest of the cost to be borne by the individual.

It was voted that dues of the Association should be increased from $20 to $25, beginning with the next fiscal year.

Nineteenth Meeting—1958

The nineteenth meeting of the American Association, on April 24-26, 1958, was the first to be held at a location other than a college campus: the meeting took place at the Willard Hotel in Washington, DC.

A portent of things to come was hinted at in the president's report for that year:

> The Southern Association of Colleges and Secondary Schools has begun admitting to full membership the institutions we represent. Someone has asked the timely question, "With the Eastern, Southern, and Central Associations operating in our region, is there a need for the the American Association?" The answer to that question is simply this: There will be no need for duplication when members of our Association can be admitted to all regional associations as equals.[32]

Other changes, too, were in the wind. In a lengthy report from Harold K. Logan on the activities of the National Federation, it was noted that some business officers advocated forming a National Association, to replace the Federation. Logan urged American Association members to consider carefully such a change.

In a report on an Executive Committee meeting, it was indicated that revision was already being considered for Volumes I and II of *College & University Business Administration*, and that the American Association would be asked to participate in the work.

A second resolution approved the modification of the bylaws of the American Association to the effect that no president should serve more than three years.

Twentieth Meeting—1959

On April 23-25, 1959, Tuskegee Institute hosted an American Association meeting for the second time.

A proposal from the National Federation that a permanent office be established for the Federation was discussed, and unanimous approval was given the proposal.

A special resolution was adopted, concerning Luther H. Foster, Sr., deceased, one of the Association founders:

> We, the members of the American Association of College Business Officers, on this our twentieth anniversary, wish to pay tribute to our friend, one of our Founders, and our first President, Luther Hilton Foster, Senior.
>
> The warmth of his personality, his efficiency, and executive ability were some of the many factors of his success. These traits were so outstanding that the General Education Board incorporated his services in determining institutions for special appropriations and fellowships. Our institutions were suffering from lack of efficient business management and the General Education Board instituted a training program at Virginia State College for potential business leaders.
>
> This, in turn, led to the development of the ideals and practices which we are still in the process of achieving. Our internship program has provided for the gradual reorganization of business practices.
>
> His ability and his achievement were so great that officials of the State of Virginia elevated him to the Presidency of the Virginia State College.
>
> His life should be an inspiration to all men.[33]

The new decade of the 1960s would bring about the dissolution of the American Association. Several factors helped to end the need for a segregated association: the hopes and determination of the early 1940s; the changes that had gathered momentum during World War II, as blacks gained new opportunities and their institutions grew to meet their needs; the force of legislation and court decisions in the 1950s; and finally, the emergence in the 1960s of a social conscience.

References—Chapter 5

1. 1950 Proceedings, p. 57.
2. 1961 Proceedings.
3. George N. Redd, Fisk University, "Current Legislative Developments of Significance to Higher Education," 1950 Proceedings, p. 49.
4. Ibid., p. 50.
5. Ibid., p. 51.
6. Preston C. Johnson, Virginia State College, "Current Legislative Developments of Significance to Higher Education," 1951 Proceedings, p. 20.
7. Ibid., p. 27.
8. Walter G. Daniel, U.S. Office of Education, "Current Legislative Developments of Significance to Higher Education," 1952 Proceedings, p. 58.
9. Lloyd E. Blauch, U.S. Office of Education, "The Administration Education Proposals," 1958 Proceedings, p. 42.
10. Byron Donegas, U.S. Office of Education, "An Address on the National Defense Education Act," 1959 Proceedings, p. 67.
11. Neal O. Hines, *Business Officers in Higher Education: A History of NACUBO* (Washington, DC: NACUBO, 1982), p. 17.
12. Jamie R. Anthony, Georgia Institute of Technology, "Appendix B, National Federation of College Business Officers Associations—Report of the President," 1952 Proceedings, pp. 85-86.
13. Hines, *A History of NACUBO*, p. 18.
14. 1955 Proceedings, p. 102.
15. 1958 Proceedings, p. 112.
16. Ibid.
17. 1950 Proceedings, p. 57.
18. Neal O. Hines, "Preface to the Third Edition," *College & University Business Administration*, 4th ed. (Washington, DC: NACUBO, 1982), p. xvi.

19. Ibid.

20. Harold K. Logan, Tuskegee Institute, "Review of *College & University Business Administration*, Volume II," 1955 Proceedings, p. 55.

21. A.W. Peterson, University of Wisconsin, "Appendix A: Report to the American Association of College Business Officers on the Preparation of a Manual on College and University Business Administration," 1952 Proceedings, p. 83.

22. 1953 Proceedings, p. 77.

23. Charles E. Prothro, Jr., Tuskegee Institute, "Progress Report: Intern Training for College Business Officers," 1955 Proceedings, p. 92.

24. American Association archives, Tuskegee Institute.

25. 1950 Proceedings, p. 57.

26. Material provided by Fisk University.

27. 1950 Proceedings, p. 57.

28. Material provided by Virginia State University.

29. Information provided by McGraw-Hill.

30. 1954 Proceedings, p. 80.

31. W.C. Ervin, Arkansas AM&N, President's Address, 1955 Proceedings, pp. 84-85.

32. William M. Jones, North Carolina College, Report of the President, 1958 Proceedings, p. 92.

33. 1959 Proceedings, pp. 95-96.

6

The Need Fulfilled: 1960-1967

For institutions and business officers throughout the country, the 1960s brought continued expansion in enrollments (as the "baby boom" generation that followed the war years reached the campus), increased federal student aid, and a growing involvement with the federal government in research grants and contracts. New technology was affecting all areas of life as the computer age arrived and electronic data processing began to be used in institutional operations. Professional development of business officers grew in importance as the role of administrators became more complex, demanding new knowledge in a variety of areas and adding both broader and deeper responsibility to their position in the institution.

For members of the American Association, the 1960s would be an especially eventful decade. The Association would celebrate its twenty-fifth anniversary in 1964. It would be involved in the metamorphosis of the National Federation of College and University Business Officers Associations into a National Association, and it would take part in a revision of *College & University Business Administration*. Finally, and of greatest importance, the organization itself would cease to exist in 1967 when, at its twenty-eighth and final meeting at North Carolina College in Durham, it would be officially dissolved. With an agreement reached by the American Association and the Southern Association in 1965—the culmination of several years of dialogue—the last barrier to full representation of black business officers in the regional associations disappeared and it became evident that the American Association had finished its task.

Topics Discussed at Meetings in the 1960s

Data Processing

Electronic data processing (EDP) appeared under four separate headings on the program of the 1960 meeting. Two speakers addressed the issue of how best to use EDP in a small institution, and others spoke on procedures for converting manual or mechanical data processing methods to electronic means and the cooperative use of equipment both within institutions and between institutions.

Robert W. Bokelman, specialist for college business management with the U.S. Department of Health, Education and Welfare, gave a presentation on using the department's tabulated institutional planning and management data as a management tool for colleges and universities. Data included information such as faculty and administrative salaries, tuition, room rates, board rates, and buildings constructed during the previous year. Bokelman returned in 1961 to speak on the same topic and added information concerning bills in Congress of interest to business officers, such as H.R. 6483, which included provisions for loans and matching grants to finance construction of college academic buildings. He added that the "College Housing Loan Program has everyone's blessing," and also that the "National Defense Education Act . . . has passed with flying colors."[1]

Business Management

Various aspects of college business management were addressed in papers given at the 1960, 1961, and 1963 meetings. Clarence Scheps, then vice president and comptroller of Tulane University, spoke on the philosophy of business management as it applies to institutions of higher education, the ends that such philosophy serves, and how to obtain efficient, sound administration. In 1961 the subject of college business management, from different viewpoints, occupied most of the program: "The Application of Basic Principles of Management to Educational Institutions" was presented by Ernest W. Walker, associate professor of finance, University of Texas; "How Can the Business Office Procedures Facilitate the Academic Program?" was delivered by Calvin L. Cooke, associate professor of accounting, Texas Southern University; and "Management of Education from a President's Point of View" was given by Samuel M. Nabrit, president, Texas Southern University.

The "Challenge of Change" was the general subject around which presentations were organized for the 1963 meeting. "The Challenge of Change in Management" was presented by Thomas E. Glaze, of the Louisiana Agricultural Experiment Station. Glaze spoke of the changes in attitude toward personnel, the need for planning, and the importance of training and of recognizing leadership qualities. He concluded by commenting, "The success or failure of university business administration in meeting the challenge of change in management may be largely determined by the quality of leadership which it puts into the effort. May history record that the college business officer was equal to the challenge."[2] Other "challenges" discussed at the meeting were coming changes in education and in accounting and budgeting.

Federal Government and Higher Education

The growing involvement of the federal government in higher education was reflected in papers given at several American Association meetings of the 1960s. In 1964 Hans Spiegel, of the Housing and Home Finance Agency, spoke on the "Future Role of the Federal Government in Higher Education," and John F. Morse, director of the Commission on Federal Relations of the American Council on Education, addressed "Special Programs and Available Grants of Governmental Agencies." The Proceedings for the 1965 meeting were never published, but in a printed meeting program located in Association archives at Tuskegee Institute, a presentation titled "Federal Support to Education for Smaller Institutions" is listed.

Two aspects of federal government involvement were addressed at the 1966 meeting: E. Bruce Heilman, then assistant vice president at George Peabody College for Teachers (and later president of the University of Richmond), spoke on "The Possible Impact of Governmental Assistance on Management in the Small College"; and a panel of speakers discussed the "Relationship of Student Financial Aid Programs to Business Management in the Small College." Heilman commented:

> It's clear that governmental assistance can make a vast difference in the future of the small college. In fact, it could be the difference between life and death for some and without doubt will be the difference between excellence and mediocrity for many. As we consider the subject at hand, we should keep in mind that to the extent a college becomes involved with the government so must

management be prepared to fulfill the accompanying requirements in administering the results of the involvement.[3]

It is interesting to note the basically optimistic attitude of Heilman
toward the impact of government aid, despite his cautionary concluding remark.

The panel on student aid gave a lengthy but cogent presentation
on federal student aid and the complications that such aid had en-
gendered in the business management of colleges and universities.
The panel discussed the consequences of the National Defense Education Act, the Economic Opportunity Act of 1964, and the Higher
Education Act of 1965.

Impact of Social Change

Frederick D. Patterson, president of the Phelps-Stokes Fund and
former president of Tuskegee Institute, spoke in 1966 on "The Impact of Social Changes on the Predominantly Negro College." Patterson maintained that the need for predominantly black institutions
still existed, in spite of the civil rights movement and a judicial end
to segregation, partly because integration was, in fact, so slow in
becoming a reality and partly because black institutions fulfilled
particular needs for some students in ways that fully integrated or
"mainstream" institutions could not.

Other Topics

In the 1960s, as in past years, certain traditional concerns of the
business officer were featured on meeting programs: accounting,
development and foundation support, physical plant, auxiliary enterprises, insurance, and retirement and annuities.

Formation of a National Association

Among the concerns of the American Association in the early
1960s was the move to replace the National Federation with a National Association. According to a report by Wendell G. Morgan,
assistant treasurer of Howard University, at the 1961 American Association meeting, a group of Federation representatives had met in
Chicago in January of that year to draw up a tentative constitution
for a National Association. At a later meeting of the Federation board
of directors, the draft of a constitution was approved and subse-

quently distributed for review to the regional associations and the American Association.

The minutes and Proceedings of the American Association for 1962 were not published, and, according to a report in the Association archives at Tuskegee Institute, the Proceedings for both 1962 and 1965 are probably "lost to posterity."[4] However, a report on the National Association in 1963 indicated that the new association had become a reality; the name had been changed from the National Federation to the National Association of College and University Business Officers and a new constitution and bylaws had been accepted. The bylaws provided that any nonprofit member of one of the four regional associations or the American Association could become a member of the National Association (indeed, membership in the national group could not be obtained without membership in one of the other five associations). However, national membership was "not mandatory for each and every regular member of a regional association."[5] The National Association's bylaws further stated that any future candidates for membership had to be from accredited, nonprofit institutions offering a bachelor's degree or higher. (As noted below, this criterion was changed in 1965 to admit two-year colleges.)

Members of the American Association supported the National Association (NACUBO) and participated in its activities. James W. Bryant of the American Association served as secretary of NACUBO from 1962 to 1965 and Burnett A. Little served in this capacity from 1965 until 1968. The American Association had been dissolved by 1968, but Harold K. Logan, a former president of the Association, served as NACUBO's secretary from 1968 until 1971.[6]

Other members of the American Association, in addition to those mentioned above, served on the board of directors of NACUBO from the time of its inception (see Appendix 4).

Support of NACUBO affected membership in the American Association. Until 1961 the membership statement of the Association had read, "Any institution doing the work of a Junior College or above may become a member by payment of the fee of $_____ annually."[7] In 1961, however, in order to bring Association membership requirements into line with those of NACUBO, the membership statement was changed as follows:

> As of May 1961, membership shall include all present members of the Association. Future applications are accepted from colleges or universities doing the work of a Bachelor's Degree or above.[8]

The statement went on to indicate that American Association members could elect to participate in NACUBO.

The level of interest in NACUBO on the part of American Association members was indicated in the 1966 American Association Proceedings by an enthusiastic report about a National Association meeting. In the report, given by R.B. Welch, then business manager of West Virginia State College and president of the American Association, reference was made to the possibility of an Esso (now Exxon) Education Foundation grant to NACUBO for the improvement of business management in predominantly black institutions. This grant and the program resulting from it would become important steps for NACUBO (see Appendix 9, "The Minority Institutions Committee of NACUBO"). The project was described in attachments to the 1967 Proceedings:

Business Management Improvement Project

One of the developments of major importance to the member institutions of the American Association of College and University Business Officers was the program of business and administrative consulting services made possible through the National Association of College and University Business Officers with grants from the Esso Education Foundation.

Early in 1967, following extended discussions and planning sessions started in 1966, the Esso Foundation made to NACUBO a grant of $50,000 to be used to provide special consulting services at five AACUBO institutions. Esso later made a second $50,000 grant to extend the services to five additional colleges.

The management consulting program incorporated five elements: (1) Visiting each campus for three to five days to review business office and related operations and to identify major problems; (2) developing plans for improvement of operations and reviewing these with the president, the business officer, and other officials; (3) establishing a timetable for implementing planned improvements; (4) making subsequent periodic visits to check progress and revise plans and target dates as necessary; and (5) submitting written reports following each visit, noting at the end of the year the progress made and plans for further work.

Peat, Marwick, Mitchell & Co. was recommended by
the Executive Committee of AACUBO and appointed by
NACUBO as the firm to render the consulting service to
the following ten colleges:

First Group:
Albany State College, Albany, Georgia
Florida Memorial College, St. Augustine, Florida
Jarvis Christian College, Hawkins, Texas
Miles College, Birmingham, Alabama
Wiley College, Marshall, Texas

Second Group:
Grambling College, Grambling, Louisiana
Huston-Tillotson College, Austin, Texas
Morehouse College, Atlanta, Georgia
Talladega College, Talladega, Alabama
Texas College, Tyler, Texas

A workshop or study seminar for all participating institutions was held on May 5-7, 1968, just before the end of
the first phase of the project. This seminar was attended
by the chief business officer, academic dean, and president
of each college. These administrative officers helped to
evaluate the results of the management improvement
project on each campus and provided a report which, it is
hoped, may serve as a guide in helping other institutions.

A similar management improvement project was initiated
by the Ford Foundation at Philander Smith College, Little
Rock, Arkansas. Plans were being formulated to extend
the management improvement program to the AACUBO
colleges not in the Esso-NACUBO pilot project.[9]

The American Association program for 1965 included a report from
Clarence Scheps, then president of NACUBO. In his talk Scheps
mentioned a move to alter the restriction on membership in NA-
CUBO in order to admit accredited junior and other two-year colleges. He indicated that the previous example of both the American
Association and the Southern Association in accepting these institutions had helped to bring about the move. In 1966 the membership
statement of the American Association once again included a reference admitting junior colleges, as had been the case prior to 1961.

MBA Program at Texas Southern University

The work of the internship program established at Tuskegee Institute in the 1950s, under auspices of the American Association, was far-reaching. Its results persuaded various individuals, such as foundation officers, that still another approach should be made to the training of college and university business officers.

In 1968 the Ford Foundation invited the School of Business of Texas Southern University (TSU) to submit a proposal for an MBA degree program in college business administration. James W. Bryant, formerly business officer at Hampton Institute and later executive vice president of the United Negro College Fund, was at least partly responsible for this invitation. Milton Wilson, who was then dean of the School of Business at TSU, was also involved. According to Wilson, at the time of the offer the TSU School of Business was the only accredited black school of business.[10]

The "rationale of the program" was given as follows:

> The shortage of managers is more acute in relation to
> Negroes trained for managerial positions. The recent em-
> phasis on recruitment of Negroes by industry, business
> and government has created severe competition in the
> employment market. Predominantly Negro colleges and
> universities find it necessary to compete in the market.
> This problem is further accentuated because these insti-
> tutions usually possess meager funds. However, their sur-
> vival relates to their ability to attract competent personnel
> to wisely manage their limited resources. Therefore, these
> institutions are in need of high-caliber managers with ed-
> ucational background and experience geared to meet the
> challenge present at these colleges and universities.[11]

The proposal was submitted, and the resulting grant provided for graduate fellowships plus dependency allowances for 30 students, library materials, visiting lectureships, travel allowances for fellows and faculty, and instructional, administrative, and clerical salaries. Between 1968 and 1971, 26 students were graduated from TSU's college business management program.

NACUBO's Black Colleges Committee, which was coming into existence even as the American Association was considering its own dissolution, also was interested in the Texas Southern program (see Appendix 9).

Revision of CUBA

Although Volume II of *College & University Business Administration* (CUBA) was not published until 1955, rapid changes in the industry indicated the need for revision of both volumes by the end of the 1950s. A "National Committee to Revise Volumes I and II, *College & University Business Administration*" was formed in 1960 under the chairmanship of Clarence Scheps, Tulane University. However, it was not until 1964, when financing was obtained, that the work proceeded under the auspices of the American Council on Education.[12] Burnett A. Little, of the American Association, was involved in the revision, which eventually was published in one volume and came to be known as *CUBA* '68.

Twenty-First Meeting—1960

Southern University extended its hospitality to the American Association a second time when the organization met there May 5-7, 1960. Reports at the meeting included a brief address by Fred S. Vorsanger, then business manager of the American Council on Education, on various ways in which the Council and the National Federation of College and University Business Officers Associations were attempting to cooperate to improve relations among the nation's business officers in higher education. He mentioned in particular a newsletter for business officers, which he himself edited; an attempt to provide a nongovernmental contact person in Washington to assist business officers with problems relating to government agencies or regulations; and provision for conferences in Washington of various business officer groups.

Dues for 1960 were listed as $20, although nothing in the minutes indicated that they had been lowered from the recent raise to $25.

Twenty-Second Meeting—1961

Texas Southern University hosted the 1961 meeting of the American Association. A report from the Association's Program and Budget Committee indicated member interest in an Association-sponsored workshop to be held in 1963 and the possibility of the Association publishing a professional journal.

A Constitution Committee, which had been appointed the previous year, presented a proposed constitution and bylaws for consideration by the membership. In this proposal (which was adopted), it was suggested that annual dues be raised to $35. (In a letter to a prospective member dated December 6, 1961, Charles E. Prothro, Jr., then secretary, indicated that $10 of annual Association dues went to membership in the National Federation.)[15] In the same proposal it was suggested that the Association name be broadened to include "University." From that time the full name was "American Association of College and University Business Officers."

Twenty-Third Meeting—1962

No Proceedings were published for the twenty-third meeting, held in 1962, but notes in the Association archives at Tuskegee Institute indicate that it took place at Fisk University, Nashville, Tennessee, on May 3-5.

Twenty-Fourth Meeting—1963

Grambling College, Grambling, Louisiana, was the site in 1963 of the twenty-fourth Association meeting. The program for that year was organized to include workshops following each address, with the speaker as workshop leader. The idea of breaking into smaller, workshop groups had been discussed for several years.

Fred S. Vorsanger, of the American Council on Education, was present again to discuss "Relationships between the Business Officer Associations and the American Council on Education." He spoke on legislative issues and national administration proposals that would affect higher education, as well as on professional development of business officers.

Twenty-Fifth Anniversary Meeting—1964

The year 1964 marked a date of particular importance to the American Association: the twenty-fifth anniversary of the organization was observed. The group met in the Statler-Hilton Hotel in Washington, DC, with Howard University, whose name appears on the Proceedings, acting as host. Howard had been the scene of the first meeting, in 1939, and this was to some extent reminiscent of that event 25 years before.

The program theme for the meeting was "Twenty-Five Years of Progress: A Foundation for Future Development,"[13] and a featured presentation was "A History of the American Association of College and University Business Officers," by James B. Clarke. In his brief account Clarke pointed out the problems that had created a need for the American Association and commented on the progress that had been made since its beginning. He said, "Our goal has always been to help provide the best educational experiences for the youth under our jurisdiction through efficient management of available resources. . . . The financial management of educational institutions has become big business that is far more complex and demanding than Negro problems per se."[14] Other topics on the program, including federal aid, auxiliary enterprises, and the business officer's responsibility in promoting excellence in education, indicated both the new problems facing business officers and the traditional issues with which they had been working since the inception of the American Association.

Twenty-Sixth Meeting—1965

No Proceedings were published for the twenty-sixth meeting of the American Association, held on May 6-8, 1965. A copy of the printed meeting program exists, however, in the Association archives and the theme is given as "Financial Assistance for the Small College." Addresses were concerned with administration, federal assistance to education, and best use of financial resources.

Twenty-Seventh Meeting—1966

The twenty-seventh meeting of the American Association took place at Florida A&M University, Tallahassee, on May 5-7, 1966. In addition to discussion of dissolution of the Association, the business session included a resolution honoring the United Negro College Fund, which, according to the 1966 Proceedings, had distributed to 33 colleges more than $90 million over the preceding 22 years. It is interesting to note how the idea of cooperative fund raising had taken hold, garnering assistance for so many institutions.

Twenty-Eighth Meeting—1967

The final meeting of the American Association of College and University Business Officers was held May 11-13, 1967, at North Carolina College, Durham, North Carolina. Don A. Davis, a founding member of the Association, was a special guest at the meeting.

The dissolution of the Association, which took place at that meeting, is covered in the concluding section of this chapter, but it may be said here that in the best and most hopeful sense the American Association had fulfilled its mission. It had provided desperately needed information and assistance, moral support, and fellowship at a time when this kind of sustenance was unavailable to black college business officers from any other source. Its officers and committee members had provided solid, worthwhile programs at the meetings; newsletters and bulletins, maintained over the years, had offered urgently needed information to members; and countless persons at various predominantly black institutions had worked behind the scenes to make Association meetings as pleasant and efficient as possible. The efforts of the Association had greatly influenced its own members and had also generally benefited the entire profession of business officers at black colleges. But now that black institutions were beginning to participate more fully in the mainstream of American higher education, and because legally based segregation was becoming a thing of the past, the American Association was no longer necessary.

Dissolution of the American Association

The possibility of dissolving the American Association had first been discussed in the decade of the 1950s (see p. 00). Certain members of the Association had joined the Central and Eastern regional groups some years before, and by the 1960s some American Association members were becoming involved with the Southern Association of College and University Business Officers (SACUBO). In the 1963 Proceedings it was mentioned that action had been taken at the 1962 meeting toward dissolving the American Association.[16]

It was not until July 13, 1965, that a decisive step was taken to admit black college business officers to full representation in SACUBO. On that date the executive committees of the American Association and the Southern Association met at the Edgewater Beach Hotel in Chicago (where they were gathered to attend a meeting of the National Association) and discussed topics relating to full acceptance of American Association members into SACUBO.

Excerpts from the "Summary of Meeting" on this historic date, obtained from records in American Association archives at Tuskegee Institute, are presented below:

The main topics discussed at the meeting were as follows:
1. Southern Association meetings to be held in cities, and in hotels, where full recognition of all members would be extended.
2. Requirements for membership in the Southern Association.

3. Ability and contributions of the representatives of all *new* members to be open for recognition. Appointment and election to committees and offices of the Southern Association to be extended on the basis of ability and the possibility of making a contribution to the effectiveness of the association.

4. Workshops for the association to be held in centers where accommodations for all participants are unrestricted.

All items discussed received a favorable response from the Southern Association officers present for the executive committees' meeting. A summary of the comments on each item follows:

Item 1. The Southern Association, in the Durham, North Carolina, 1965 meeting, passed a resolution to accept applications for membership in the Southern Association from all colleges holding membership in the regional accrediting association for their area.

This resolution removes the exclusion of the Negro colleges from membership. This information was passed on to the host college(s) for the next meeting to be held in Dallas, Texas, April 6-9, 1966, and likewise for the 1967 National Association of College and University Business Officers meeting to be held in New Orleans, Louisiana. The Southern Association will be host for the 1967 National Association meeting. Those facilities in which these meetings will be held are open for full accommodations to all representatives and their friends who will participate.

Item 2. Applications are acted upon by the secretary for the Southern Association. If the applying institution holds membership in the regional rating association, the application will be acted upon favorably.

Item 3. A favorable response was made to this statement. The recognition of the association's membership by those in position to influence decisions, regarding selection of officials, must be left to the future. Active participation in future years will provide the answer to any concern that exists in this area.

Item 4. Workshops are held in cities or on campuses and are usually of one day's duration. Housing is not required for these meetings. Where housing is required, cities in which the workshop is held will provide public accommodations that are suitable. When meals are a part of the meetings, unrestricted accommodations are recognized.

Remarks: The above summary of the items discussed is an accurate expression of the statements made by officers of the Southern Association of College and University Business Officers in attendance. These expressions, as stated, are those of a number of the major officers of the Southern Association. Your Executive Committee recognizes that except for the resolutions in reference to membership, and the request for selection of facilities to accommodate all institutional representatives in attendance, comments on other items of importance must be understood to carry only the weight of the officers in attendance. Your Executive Committee members present, hence, go on record to encourage the institutions presently members of AACUBO and located in the region from which the Southern Association draws its members to apply for membership and join the Southern Association. It is our desire that a very favorable number of AACUBO institutions will apply and have membership by the April 6-9, 1966, meeting of the Southern Association in Dallas, and be in attendance at this meeting.[17]

It should be stated here that the effort to achieve full Southern Association membership for black college business officers involved persons on both sides. Certain members of SACUBO, in particular Clarence Scheps, worked hard to change the prevailing customs of earlier times and overcome the strictures of thought left by a long history of segregation.

"Some of us recognized that the move toward integration was an idea whose time had come—it ought to be done—and the others in SACUBO went along with us," Scheps stated.[18] He was secretary of SACUBO when he proposed the interpretation of Southern Association bylaws that would leave no doubt about admitting black business officers. Excerpts from the Proceedings of the 1965 SA-CUBO Annual Meeting, at which the proposal was made, are below:

> Secretary Clarence Scheps: For a number of years, successive Executive Committees of this Association have had before them a rather serious and difficult problem that had to do with the admission of all qualified institutions in the South to membership in this Association.
>
> This problem was inevitable, and one that could be foreseen for many years, but it came to a head about four or five years ago. At this time, the American Association of College and University Business Officers, which is the Negro college counterpart of SACUBO, indicated that it wished to go out of business, stating that it was a rather anomalous regional association which came into being for historic reasons, these reasons for continued existence being no longer valid. Further, according to the American Association, as soon as membership was available to Negro institutions in all the appropriate regional associations, this association would go out of business.
>
> Your representatives on the National Board at that time replied that the reasons given by the American Association were certainly logical and understood, and that there was sympathy for this position.
>
> However, we pointed out that Southern institutions were not integrated to a large extent. Mechanically it would have been difficult to hold meetings of this Association except in one or two cities in the South, and therefore we asked the indulgence of the American Association for this subject to be studied a little more and perhaps confronted at a more timely occasion.
>
> In the opinion of your Executive Committee, the time is now. At a special meeting in Atlanta in January, the following resolution was unanimously adopted by those Executive Committee members present. It simply says this:
>
> The officers and Executive Committee of the Southern Association of College and University Business Officers will present at the next annual meeting of the Association, to be held in Durham, North Carolina, on March 31 and

April 1-2, 1965, a proposal for admitting all qualified institutions to membership in the Association.

• • • • •

Virtually all educational associations in the country except SACUBO admit all qualified institutions. . . . I think that the time has come for us to take an action which will recognize that these institutions who are our neighbors need our help, they need the association with this group, and despite problems of adjustment that this step will bring, we believe that the time has come to take the step in adjusting in this area.

My motion, Mr. President, simply is that we interpret the bylaws in a different sense than has been done traditionally by custom. A change in the bylaws is not needed because the words are all here.

Let me read that portion of the constitution and bylaws which pertains to membership. It says:

"Any responsible institution of higher education or any institution or organization determined by the Executive Committee to be primarily related to higher education may apply for membership."

To repeat: I now move that this organization, effective immediately, interpret its constitution and bylaws to mean that any qualified institution which meets the standards of the Association should be admitted to membership in the Southern Association.[19]

Scheps commented that he and his good friend, Burnie Little, had worked for years toward the dissolution of the American Association and full integration of its members into SACUBO. (As mentioned in Chapter 1, EACUBO opened its doors to all qualified institutions in 1960, and CACUBO had never refused black business officers.)

The integration of black business officers into SACUBO proved to be highly successful. Blacks participated fully in SACUBO activities, and in later years SACUBO was to elect two black presidents, both of whom served with distinction: Harold K. Logan, then of Tuskegee Institute, and Charles C. Teamer, of Dillard University.

With the reaching of the 1965 agreement between the American and Southern Associations, it was felt that the need for the American

Association had ended, and that to perpetuate the Association would be to continue a segregated group, which was against the principles for which American Association members had struggled so long. Therefore, it was determined that the American Association should be dissolved.

In the minutes of an American Association Executive Committee meeting of February 11, 1967, mention is made of a report by Paul G. King, business manager at Tennessee A&I University, on the proposed dissolution. At the same Executive Committee meeting, Augustus L. (Gus) Palmer suggested that August 31, 1967, should be the official date of dissolution, to which the rest of the committee agreed.

The 1967 meeting of the full Association—the final meeting—took place in May, at which time appreciation was expressed to members of the Dissolution Committee, which had prepared the Resolution for Dissolution (see Appendix 6). The committee was chaired by Harold K. Logan, its other members being G. Leon Netterville; William M. Jones, vice president for finance, North Carolina College; Glenwood E. Jones, director of buildings and grounds, Virginia State College; Paul G. King; Isaiah T. Creswell; and A.L. Palmer.

The Dissolution Resolution indicated that the American Association had had 82 members at its peak, including institutions from the District of Columbia, Pennsylvania, Missouri, and the 17 Southern states. It affirmed that Association papers and records would be kept as archives at Tuskegee Institute, and that the balance on hand in the Association treasury, after all obligations had been met, would be donated to NACUBO, for the purpose "of improving business management in predominantly Negro colleges" (see Appendix 7).

The Resolution also contained a provision for writing the history of the American Association of College and University Business Officers. Although more research can still be done, it is hoped that with this writing the obligation has been fulfilled.

References—Chapter 6

1. Robert W. Bokelman, Department of Health, Education and Welfare, "Utilization of College Planning and Management Data," 1961 Proceedings, p. 60.
2. Thomas E. Glaze, Louisiana Agricultural Experiment Station, "The Challenge of Change in Management," 1963 Proceedings, p. 26.

3. E. Bruce Heilman, George Peabody College for Teachers, "The Possible Impact of Governmental Assistance on Management in the Small College," 1966 Proceedings, pp. 27-28.

4. Report of the Secretary, May 12, 1967, American Association archives, Tuskegee Institute.

5. Report on the National Association, 1963 Proceedings, p. 54.

6. Neal O. Hines, *Business Officers in Higher Education: A History of NACUBO* (Washington, DC: NACUBO, 1982), pp. 98-99.

7. 1960 Proceedings, p. 7.

8. 1961 Proceedings, p. ii.

9. 1967 Proceedings, pp. 117-119.

10. Milton Wilson, Howard University, interview with author.

11. "Proposal: College Business Officers Program, School of Business, Texas Southern University." Material provided by A. L. Palmer, Howard University.

12. Neal O. Hines, "Preface to the Third Edition," *College & University Business Administration*, 4th ed. (Washington, DC: NACUBO, 1982), p. xvii.

13. 1964 Proceedings, p. x.

14. James B. Clarke, Howard University, "History of the American Association of College and University Business Officers," 1964 Proceedings, p. 6.

15. Charles E. Prothro, Jr., letter to prospective Association member, December 6, 1961, American Association archives, Tuskegee Institute.

16. 1963 Proceedings, p. 60.

17. "Summary of Meeting, Executive Committees, American and Southern Associations, July 13, 1965, Chicago, Illinois," American Association archives, Tuskegee Institute.

18. Clarence Scheps, interview with author.

19. 1965 SACUBO Proceedings, pp. 136-138.

Appendixes

1: Purpose

The purpose as originally stated was as follows:

> To secure closer association for the personnel and for member institutions for discussion of mutual problems and to secure the advancement of professional standards among those responsible for business administration of these institutions.

The purpose was changed in the bylaws adopted May 1961, and expanded as follows:

> (1) To secure closer association for members and member institutions for discussion of mutual problems and to give organized and effective direction to the development of improved principles and practices of educational business administration in order that the members may serve more efficiently the educational objectives of their institutions.

> (2) To afford opportunity for acquaintance and friendship among college and university business officers in order that they may develop and maintain educational business administration as a profession with professional ideals and standards.

> (3) To secure the advancement of professional standards among those responsible for the business administration of their institutions.

> (4) To provide opportunities for effective concerted action in all matters affecting the financial welfare of institutions of higher education.

> (5) To select and disseminate among the membership new and useful information.

2: The Charter Members

Alcorn Agricultural & Mechanical
College
Alcorn, MS
H. W. Norris, *Financial Secretary*

Arkansas Agricultural, Mechanical
& Normal College
Pine Bluff, AR
Frank B. Adair, *Accountant*

Bennett College
Greensboro, NC
Flemmie P. Kittrell, *Dean of
Students*

Bluefield State Teachers College
Bluefield, WV
R. R. Carroll, *Financial Secretary*

Cheyney Training School for
Teachers
Cheyney, PA
Mrs. L. N. Conway, *Bursar*

Dover State College for Colored
Students
Dover, DE
James B. Clarke, *Business Manager*

Florida Agricultural & Mechanical
College for Negroes
Tallahassee, FL
J. R. E. Lee, Jr., *Business Manager*

Hampton Institute
Hampton, VA
Robert O. Purves, *Treasurer*
Don A. Davis, *Cashier & Chief
Accountant*
W. E. Carter, *Director of Trade
School*

Howard University
Washington, DC
V. D. Johnston, *Treasurer*
Gustav Auzenne, Jr., *Assistant
Treasurer*
Luther H. Foster, Jr., *Budget
Officer*
D. W. Edmonds, *Cashier*
L. L. Whaley, *Purchasing Agent*
E. S. Hope, *Supt. of Buildings and
Grounds*
Gwendolyn C. Goldston, *Mgr.
Dining Halls*
Alida P. Banks, *Acting Dean of
Women*

Johnson C. Smith University
Charlotte, NC
Wendell G. Morgan, *Business
Manager*

Lincoln University
Chester County, PA
Susan Lighston, *Dietitian*

Lincoln University
Jefferson City, MO
J. T. Johnson, *Accountant*

Morgan State College
Baltimore, MD
James H. Carter, *Secretary-
Business Manager*

Morris Brown University
Atlanta, GA
W. A. Hamilton, *Business Officer*

North Carolina Agricultural &
  Technical College
Greensboro, NC
N.C. Webster, *Bursar & Asst. Bus.*
  Manager

North Carolina College for
  Negroes
Durham, NC
Charles C. Amey, *Business*
  Manager

Shaw University
Raleigh, NC
Glenwood E. Jones, *Business*
  Manager

Southern University
Scotlandville, LA
G. Leon Netterville, *Business*
  Manager

State Colored Normal, Industrial,
  Agricultural & Mechanical
  College of South Carolina
Orangeburg, SC
J. I. Washington, *Business Manager*

Tuskegee Institute
Tuskegee, AL
Lloyd Isaacs, *Treasurer*
Edmond Burke, *Comptroller*

Virginia State College
Petersburg, VA
Luther H. Foster, Sr., *Treasurer-*
  Business Mgr.
James B. Cephas, *Bookkeeper*

Virginia Union University
Richmond, VA
E. M. Frazier, *Bursar*
L. W. Davis, *Director, Student*
  Employment

West Virginia State College
Institute, WV
C. R. Rutherford, *Business*
  Manager
Newman Goldston, *Superintendent*

Wilberforce University
Wilberforce, OH
G. H. Valentine, *Secretary-*
  Treasurer

Wiley College
Marshall, TX
Harold K. Logan, *Business Manager*

3: All Institutions That Were Members of the American Association

Alabama Agricultural and
  Mechanical University,
  Normal, AL
Alabama State University,
  Montgomery, AL
Albany State College, Albany, GA
Alcorn State University,
  Lorman, MS
Allen University, Columbia, SC
Arkansas AM&N College, Pine
  Bluff, AR
Atlanta University, Atlanta, GA
Benedict College, Columbia, SC
Bennett College, Greensboro, NC
Bethune Cookman College,
  Daytona Beach, FL
Bishop College, Dallas, TX
Bluefield State College,
  Bluefield, WV
Central State University,
  Wilberforce, OH
Cheyney University of
  Pennsylvania, Cheyney, PA
Claflin College, Orangeburg, SC
Clark College, Atlanta, GA
Delaware State College, Dover, DE
Dillard University,
  New Orleans, LA
Edward Waters College,
  Jacksonville, FL
Elizabeth City State University,
  Elizabeth City, NC
Fayetteville State College,
  Fayetteville, NC
Fisk University, Nashville, TN
Florida A&M University,
  Tallahassee, FL
Florida Normal and Industrial
  Institute, St. Augustine, FL
Fort Valley State College,
  Fort Valley, GA
Gammon Theological Seminary,
  Atlanta, GA
Georgia State College,
  Savannah, GA

Gibbs Junior College,
  St. Petersburg, FL
Grambling State University,
  Grambling, LA
Hampton University,
  Hampton, VA
Howard University,
  Washington, DC
Huston-Tillotson College,
  Austin, TX
Interdenominational Theological
  Center, Atlanta, GA
Jackson State University,
  Jackson, MS
Jarvis Christian College,
  Hawkins, TX
Johnson C. Smith University,
  Charlotte, NC
J. P. Campbell College,
  Jackson, MS
Kansas Technical Institute,
  Topeka, KS
Kentucky State University,
  Frankfort, KY
Knoxville College, Knoxville, TN
Langston University, Langston, OK
Leland College, Baker, LA
Le Moyne-Owen College,
  Memphis, TN
Lincoln University,
  Chester County, PA
Lincoln University,
  Jefferson City, MO
Livingstone College, Salisbury, NC
Maryland State College, Princess
  Anne County, MD
Meharry Medical College,
  Nashville, TN
Miles College, Birmingham, AL
Mississippi Valley State
  University, Itta Bena, MS
Morehouse College, Atlanta, GA
Morgan State University,
  Baltimore, MD
Morris Brown College, Atlanta, GA

Morris College, Sumter, SC
Morristown College,
  Morristown, TN
North Carolina Agricultural and
  Technical State University,
  Greensboro, NC
North Carolina State College,
  Durham, NC
Okolona College, Okolona, MS
Paine College, Augusta, GA
Philander Smith College,
  Little Rock, AR
Prairie View A&M University,
  Prairie View, TX
Rust College, Holly Springs, MS
Saint Augustine's College,
  Raleigh, NC
Savannah State College,
  Savannah, GA
Shaw University, Raleigh, NC
South Carolina State College,
  Orangeburg, SC
Southern University Agricultural
  and Mechanical College,
  Baton Rouge, LA
Spelman College, Atlanta, GA
Saint Paul's College,
  Lawrenceville, VA
Storer College, Harpers Ferry, WV

Talladega College, Talladega, AL
Tennessee State University,
  Nashville, TN
Texas College, Tyler, TX
Texas Southern University,
  Houston, TX
Tougaloo College, Tougaloo, MS
Tuskegee Institute, Tuskegee
  Institute, AL
Utica Junior College—Campus,
  Utica, MS
Virginia State University,
  Petersburg, VA
Virginia State College, Norfolk, VA
Virginia Union University,
  Richmond, VA
Voorhees College, Denmark, SC
West Virginia State College,
  Institute, WV
Wilberforce University,
  Wilberforce, OH
Wiley College, Marshall, TX
Winston-Salem State University,
  Winston-Salem, NC
Xavier University of Louisiana,
  New Orleans, LA

United Negro College Fund,
  New York, NY

4: Officers of the American Association, 1939-1967

No.	Year	Place	Officers	Executive Committee	Placement Officer
1	1939	Howard University Washington, D.C.	Luther H. Foster, Sr., Pres. J. R. E. Lee, Jr., Vice Pres. V. D. Johnston, Secy. C. R. Rutherford, Treas.	Harold K. Logan Edmond H. Burke Robert O. Purves	None
2	1940	Tuskegee Institute Tuskegee, Alabama	Luther H. Foster, Sr., Pres. J. R. E. Lee, Jr., Vice Pres. V. D. Johnston, Secy. C. R. Rutherford, Treas.	Harold K. Logan Edmond H. Burke Robert O. Purves	None
3	1941	Bluefield State College Bluefield, West Virginia	Don A. Davis, Pres. Jesse F. Beals, Vice Pres. V. D. Johnston, Secy. Glenwood E. Jones, Treas.	J. R. E. Lee, Jr. W. A. Hamilton	Luther H. Foster, Sr.
4	1942	Bennett College Greensboro, North Carolina	Don A. Davis, Pres. Jesse F. Beals, Vice Pres. V. D. Johnston, Secy. Glenwood E. Jones, Treas.	J. V. Anderson Charles C. Avery	Luther H. Foster, Sr.
5	1943	No Meeting	Same	Same	Same
6	1944	Hampton Institute Hampton, Virginia	Don A. Davis, Pres. A. H. Turner, Vice Pres. V. D. Johnston, Secy. Glenwood E. Jones, Treas.	Charles C. Avery J. V. Anderson	Luther H. Foster, Sr.
6	1945	Southern University Baton Rouge, Louisiana	G. L. Netterville, Pres. C. R. Rutherford, Vice Pres. V. D. Johnston, Secy. W. A. Hamilton, Treas.	J. V. Anderson Mrs. W. D. Clayton Don A. Davis	Luther H. Foster, Sr.

No.	Year	Place	Officers	Executive Committee	Placement Officer	Federation Representatives
7	1946	Shaw University Raleigh, North Carolina	G. L. Netterville, Pres. I. T. Creswell, Vice Pres. V. D. Johnston, Secy. M. G. Birchette, Treas.	Don A. Davis Viola Means W. G. Morgan	Luther H. Foster, Sr.	None
8	1947	Wiley and Bishop Colleges Marshall, Texas	V.D. Johnston, Pres. A. I. Terrell, Vice Pres. L. H. Foster, Jr., Secy. M. G. Birchette, Treas.	Don A. Davis H. J. Mason G. L. Netterville	Luther H. Foster, Sr.	None
9	1948	Florida A&M College Tallahassee, Florida	V. D. Johnston, Pres. A. I. Terrell, Vice Pres. L. H. Foster, Jr., Secy. M. G. Birchette, Treas.	Don A. Davis Lloyd Isaacs G. L. Netterville	Luther H. Foster, Sr.	None
10	1949	Atlanta University and Clark, Spelman, Morehouse, and Morris Brown Colleges Atlanta, Georgia	V. D. Johnston, President A. I. Terrell, Vice Pres. L. H. Foster, Jr., Secy. M. G. Birchette, Treas.	Don A. Davis Lloyd Isaacs G. L. Netterville	Luther H. Foster, Sr.	None

No.	Year	Place	Officers	Executive Committee	Placement Officer	Federation Representatives
11	1950	Fisk University and Tennessee A&I College Nashville, Tennessee	A. I. Terrell, Pres. W. A. Hamilton, Vice Pres. L. H. Foster, Jr., Secy. M. G. Birchette, Treas.	W. C. Ervin G. L. Netterville C. E. Prothro, Jr.	Don A. Davis	None
12	1951	Virginia State College Petersburg, Virginia	W. A. Hamilton, Pres. Glenwood E. Jones, Vice Pres. L. H. Foster, Jr., Secy. S. F. Lynem, Treas.	I. T. Creswell A. A. Reid A. I. Terrell	Don A. Davis	None
13	1952	Kentucky State College Frankfort, Kentucky	G. E. Jones, Pres. J. R. E. Lee, Jr., Vice Pres. L. H. Foster, Jr., Secy. S. F. Lynem, Treas.	W. A. Hamilton J. B. Cephas W. S. Clayton	Don A. Davis	Glenwood E. Jones Luther H. Foster, Jr.
14	1953	Ft. Valley State College Fort Valley, Georgia	J. R. E. Lee, Jr., Pres. J. B. Cephas, Vice Pres. L. H. Foster, Jr., Secy. S. F. Lynem, Treas.	R. H. Beasley G. E. Jones P. J. Lee	Don A. Davis	J. R. E. Lee, Jr. Luther H. Foster, Jr.

No.	Year	Place	Officers	Executive Committee	Placement Officer	Federation Representatives
15	1954	Lincoln University Jefferson City, Missouri	J. B. Cephas, Pres. S. F. Lynem, Vice Pres. L. H. Foster, Jr., Secy. W. M. Jones, Treas.	L. R. Bywaters J. R. E. Lee, Jr. Deryck Weaver	Don A. Davis	J. B. Cephas Luther H. Foster, Jr.
16	1955	Arkansas AM&N College Pine Bluff, Arkansas	W. C. Ervin, Pres. J. B. Clarke, Vice Pres. B. A. Little, Secy. W. M. Jones, Treas.	J. W. Bryant G. H. Valentine J. B. Cephas	Don A. Davis	W. C. Ervin B. A. Little
17	1956	Winston-Salem Teachers College Winston-Salem, North Carolina	J. B. Clarke, Pres. H. K. Logan, Vice Pres. B. A. Little, Secy. G. H. Valentine, Treas.	W. C. Ervin H. H. Gunn C. A. Christopher	Don A. Davis	James B. Clarke B. A. Little
18	1957	Hampton Institute Hampton, Virginia	H. K. Logan, Pres. W. M. Jones, Vice Pres. B. A. Little, Secy. G. H. Valentine, Treas.	J. B. Clarke S. V. Jeter Paul G. King	Don A. Davis	Harold K. Logan B. A. Little
19	1958	The Willard Hotel Washington, D.C.	W. M. Jones, Pres. W. G. Morgan, Vice Pres. S. V. Jeter, Secy. G. Cletus Birchette, Treas.	H. K. Logan L. R. Bywaters A. S. Parks	Don A. Davis	William M. Jones S. V. Jeter Wendell G. Morgan

No.	Year	Place	Officers	Executive Committee	Placement Officer	Federation Representatives
20	1959	Tuskegee Institute Tuskegee, Alabama	W. G. Morgan, Pres. Paul G. King, Vice Pres. S. V. Jeter, Secy. Mrs. J. D. Carlton, Asst. Sec. G. Cletus Birchette, Treas.	W. M. Jones E. D. Draper A. W. Eason	Harold K. Logan	Wendell G. Morgan S. V. Jeter Paul G. King

No.	Year	Place	Officers	Executive Committee	Placement Officer	National Association Representatives
21	1960	Southern University Baton Rouge, Louisiana	Paul G. King, Pres. G. Cletus Birchette, Vice Pres. S. V. Jeter, Secy. A. L. Palmer, Asst. Secy. C. E. Prothro, Jr., Treas.	G. A. Owens W. A. Morgan M. A. Johnson	Harold K. Logan	Paul G. King S. V. Jeter W. G. Morgan
22	1961	Texas Southern University Houston, Texas	G. C. Birchette, Pres. I. T. Creswell, Vice Pres. C. E. Prothro, Jr., Secy. A. L. Palmer, Asst. Secy. C. W. Moore, Treas.	Paul G. King E. A. Bertrand M. A. Johnson	Harold K. Logan	G. C. Birchette C. E. Prothro, Jr., W. G. Morgan

No.	Year	Place	Officers	Executive Committee	Placement Officer	National Association Representatives
23	1962	Fisk University Nashville, Tennessee	I. T. Creswell, Pres. M. A. Johnson, Vice Pres. C. E. Prothro, Jr., Secy. A. L. Palmer, Asst. Secy. C. W. Moore, Treas.	G. C. Birchette R. B. Welch L. P. Chambliss	Harold K. Logan	I. T. Creswell G. C. Birchette C. E. Prothro, Jr.
24	1963	Grambling College Grambling, Louisiana	I. T. Creswell, Pres. A. L. Palmer, Vice Pres. J. W. Bryant, Secy. O. L. Brandon, Asst. Secy. C. W. Moore, Treas.	J. A. Ramas A. J. Pindle	Harold K. Logan	I. T. Creswell J. W. Bryant W. G. Morgan
25	1964	Statler Hilton Hotel Washington, D.C.	A. L. Palmer, Pres. J. W. Bryant, Vice Pres. O. L. Brandon, Secy. E. J. Junior, Jr., Asst. Secy. C. W. Moore, Treas.	I. T. Creswell H. R. Alexander W. E. McNeal	Harold K. Logan	A. L. Palmer J. W. Bryant I. T. Creswell
26	1965	Atlanta University Atlanta, Georgia	J. W. Bryant, Pres. R. B. Welch, Vice Pres. E. J. Junior, Jr., Secy. M. M. Nance, Asst. Secy. C. W. Moore, Treas.	A. L. Palmer G. C. Birchette L. D. Smith	Harold K. Logan	A. L. Palmer B. A. Little J. W. Bryant

No.	Year	Place	Officers	Executive Committee	Placement Officer	National Association Representatives
27	1966	Florida A&M University Tallahassee, Florida	R. B. Welch, Pres. B. A. Little, Vice Pres. E. J. Junior, Jr., Secy. M. M. Nance, Asst. Secy. C. W. Moore, Treas.	H. R. Partridge J. V. Parham	Harold K. Logan	R. B. Welch B. A. Little M. M. Nance
28	1967	North Carolina College Durham, North Carolina	B. A. Little, Pres.* M. M. Nance, Vice Pres. E. J. Junior, Jr., Secy. E. W. Johnson, Asst. Secy. M. J. Bergeron, Treas.	R. B. Welch W. M. Jones J. V. Parham	Harold K. Logan	B. A. Little R. B. Welch M. M. Nance
Dissolution:			Same	Same	Same	Same

*The same persons were continued in office for 1967-1968 to carry out the dissolution measures outlined in the Resolution approved on May 13, 1967, at the Twenty-Eighth and final meeting of the Association.

5: Bylaws of the American Association of College and University Business Officers Adopted May, 1961

Article I
Name and Purpose
Section 1. Name
The name of this organization is: THE AMERICAN ASSOCIATION OF COLLEGE AND UNIVERSITY BUSINESS OFFICERS.

Section 2. Purpose
The purpose of this Association shall be as follows:

(1) To secure closer association for members and member institutions for discussion of mutual problems and to give organized and effective direction to the development of improved principles and practices of educational business administration in order that the members may serve more efficiently the educational objectives of their institutions.

(2) To afford opportunity for acquaintance and friendship among college and university business officers in order that they may develop and maintain educational business administration as a profession with professional ideals and standards.

(3) To secure the advancement of professional standards among those responsible for the business administration of their institutions.

(4) To provide opportunities for effective concerted action in all matters affecting the financial welfare of institutions of higher education.

(5) To select and disseminate among the membership new and useful information.

Article II
Membership and Dues
Section 1. Membership
Membership shall be limited to:

(a) All present members.
(b) Any institution doing work of a Bachelor's Degree or above, or any individual or institution so voted by the majority of the members in regular session.

Section 2. Dues
The annual dues of the Association will be $35, institutional branches shall be considered to be separate fees and so billed. Branch institutions have the same voting rights and privileges as parent institutions.

Section 3. If a member institution should become two years delinquent in the payment of dues, the secretary of the Association shall give that school written notice of the delinquency and, after a month's grace period, drop said school from the membership roster.

Delinquent schools will be permitted to reinstate by paying dues for the current year and a reinstatement fee equal to the current dues.

Article III
Officers
Section 1. The officers of this Association shall be a President, a Vice President, a Secretary, an Assistant Secretary, a Treasurer, and a Placement Officer, who shall be elected at the close of each annual meeting for a term of one year or until their successors are elected.

Section 2. The President shall be the executive officer of the Association and shall be responsible to the Executive Committee for the general supervision and direction of the affairs of the Association. He shall preside at all meetings of the Association and of the Executive Committee.

Section 3. In the event of absence or incapacity of the President or the vacancy of the office of the President, the Vice President shall occupy the office and assume the functions of the President as herein stated until his successor is elected.

Section 4. The Secretary shall give notice of all meetings of the Association and the Executive Committee and shall keep the minutes of such meetings; he shall be responsible for the records other than financial of the Association and for conducting its correspondence; under the direction of the President and the Executive Committee he shall make the necessary arrangements for a place of the meeting for the Executive Committee and for the annual meeting of the Association. He shall be responsible for the printing of the proceedings, official stationery and the distributing of the same. He shall be responsible for getting out the Newsletter and other news media to the membership.

Section 5. The Assistant Secretary shall perform those functions as assigned by the President or the Secretary. In general, these functions would be in the way of assistance to the Secretary.

Section 6. The Treasurer shall be bonded and shall have custody of all of the funds of the Association; he shall be responsible for the collection of dues and other monies due the Association and subject to the action of the Executive Committee for the approval of the disbursement of funds; and he shall keep adequate records of receipt and disbursement of funds and shall report thereon at the request of the President or Executive Committee and at the annual meeting of the Association.

Article IV
The Executive Committee
The Executive Committee shall consist of the President, the Vice President, the Secretary, the Assistant Secretary, the Treasurer, the Placement Officers, all ex officio, and three other members elected for a term of one year each—none of the three being eligible to succeed himself.

The Executive Committee shall be the governing body of the Association and shall have full power to do all things necessary to carry out the Association's objectives and purposes including the power to fill any vacancies in the Executive Committee which may occur between annual meetings. In so doing the Executive Committee shall be empowered within the resources available to make commitments, financial and otherwise, on behalf of the Association.

Article V
Meetings of the Association
Section 1. An annual meeting of the Association shall be held as determined by the vote of the Executive Committee.

Section 2. Special meetings may be called by the Executive Committee provided written notice is sent to each member institution at least thirty days prior thereto.

Article VI
Committees
The President shall appoint the following committees consisting of chairman and five members each: an Auditing Committee; a Nominating Committee; a Resolutions Committee; and a Time and Place Committee. Reports from these committees will be made at the business session of the annual meeting. Special-purpose committees may be appointed from time to time by the President to serve until the annual election.

Article VII
Nominations and Elections
The Nominating Committee shall propose a slate of officers, and members of the Executive Committee to be voted upon at the annual business meeting. Prior to the voting on the slate proposed by the Nominating Committee, an opportunity shall be given by the President for nominations for any office from the floor. Elections shall be by voice vote except that if there should be a nomination from the floor a ballot election shall be held.

Article VIII
Voting
For the purposes of voting, including the annual election, each member institution shall be entitled to one vote. Member institutions will determine

the representative to cast their votes where more than one person holds membership with the Association.

Article IX
Amendments
These By-Laws may be amended at any regular or special meeting, properly called, by a two-thirds vote of the members present provided thirty days' notice of any proposed amendment shall have been sent to each member institution.

6: Members of the Dissolution Committee

Harold K. Logan, Tuskegee Institute, *Chairman*
I.T. Creswell, Fisk University
Glenwood E. Jones, Virginia State College
William M. Jones, North Carolina College
Paul G. King, Tennessee A&I University
G. Leon Netterville, Southern University
A.L. Palmer, Texas Southern University

7: Dissolution Resolution

RESOLUTION

WHEREAS, THE AMERICAN ASSOCIATION OF COLLEGE AND UNI-VERSITY BUSINESS OFFICERS, an unincorporated association (formerly known as the Association of Business Officers in Schools for Negroes), was organized in the year of 1939 by various educational institutions at Howard University, Washington, D.C., and

WHEREAS, The founding institutions of the Association were Negro colleges, and

WHEREAS, At the time of the Association's organization, the existing regional associations of college and university business officers would not receive into membership business officers serving Negro colleges unless the officers were of the white race, and

WHEREAS, The Association has grown from the four founding institutions to eighty-two (82) colleges and universities located throughout seventeen (17) southern states, the District of Columbia, Missouri and Pennsylvania; and has carried out admirably the purposes for which it was formed, and

WHEREAS, The bars to membership of Negroes heretofore existing in the regional associations of college and university business officers have largely disappeared, and

WHEREAS, A duly appointed committee of the Association was formed to study the problem of whether the Association could carry out best its purpose under its present organization, and

WHEREAS, The said committee, designated the Dissolution Committee, after investigation and due deliberation, met on February 10, 1967, at the Voyager Inn in Durham, North Carolina, and

WHEREAS, At said meeting, the delegates thereto, being of the opinion that the professional objectives of the membership would be served best by a dissolution of the said Association, did adopt a resolution recommending to the members of the Association that the organization be dissolved, and

WHEREAS, The governing body of the Association, its Executive Committee, subsequently approved the said resolution of the Dissolution Committee in all respects and adopted the same as its own resolution, and

WHEREAS, The resolution of the Dissolution Committee contained certain measures to be carried out pursuant to dissolution, which measures are immediately hereinafter set forth:

1) That all obligations of the Association be taken care of before any disposition is made of remaining funds.

2) That funds in the amount of $_____ be made available for the writing of the history of the Association.

3) That the balance on hand, after all obligations have been taken care of, be donated to the National Association of College and University Business Officers for the purpose of improving business management in predominantly Negro colleges. (Initially a pilot group of five [5] institutions will be involved; however, the program will be expanded and conducted on a continuing basis. We recommend that there be a tie between this project and the Intern Training Program for Business Management at Tuskegee Institute.)

4) That the papers and records of the Association be permanently deposited in the Library at Tuskegee Institute.

5) That no later than October 1, 1967, the Executive Committee advise all National and Regional professional organizations, with which the Association has had some connection, as to the dissolution of the American Association of College and University Business Officers.

And,

WHEREAS, At its spring meeting held at Durham, North Carolina, on _____ , 1967, the Association in solemn assembly convened, the members thereof having had due notice of the recommended dissolution, and being otherwise fully advised in the premises, after due deliberation and roll call vote, did by two-thirds (2/3) vote, approve and adopt the recommendations and report of the Dissolution Committee.

NOW, THEREFORE BE IT RESOLVED, That THE AMERICAN ASSOCIATION OF COLLEGE AND UNIVERSITY BUSINESS OFFICERS shall be forever dissolved, effective August 31, 1967.

BE IT FURTHER RESOLVED, That the Executive Committee is hereby empowered to carry out the liquidation and dissolution measures as outlined in its dissolution plan and herein above detailed.

BE IT FURTHER RESOLVED, That on or before December 1, 1967, the said Executive Committee shall make its report to the membership on the implementation of the dissolution plan.

ATTEST:_____   _____

Secretary, AMERICAN   President, AMERICAN
ASSOCIATION OF COLLEGE   ASSOCIATION OF COLLEGE
AND UNIVERSITY   AND UNIVERSITY
BUSINESS OFFICERS   BUSINESS OFFICERS

I, ———————————————————— , Secretary of THE AMERICAN ASSOCIATION OF COLLEGE AND UNIVERSITY BUSINESS OFFICERS, do hereby certify that at its annual meeting held at ——————————— ——————————————— , on ——————————— , 1967, a quorum being present, the above and foregoing resolution was adopted by two-thirds (2/3) vote of the members of said organization.

————————————————————
Secretary
THE AMERICAN
ASSOCIATION OF COLLEGE
AND UNIVERSITY
BUSINESS OFFICERS

8: Members of the American Association Who Became College or University Presidents

Member	Institution of Which He Became President
Luther H. Foster, Sr.	Virginia State University (formerly College), Petersburg, Virginia
Luther H. Foster, Jr.	Tuskegee Institute, Tuskegee, Alabama
Wright L. Lassiter, Jr.	Bishop College, Dallas, Texas
Alonzo G. Moron	Hampton Institute, Hampton, Virginia
M. Maceo Nance, Jr.	South Carolina State College, Orangeburg, South Carolina
G. Leon Netterville	Southern University, Baton Rouge, Louisiana
George A. Owens	Tougaloo, College, Tougaloo, Mississippi

9: The Minority Institutions Committee of NACUBO

NACUBO's Minority Institutions Committee had its beginnings in an ad hoc group called the "Steering Committee on Improvements in Business Management at the Predominantly Negro Colleges," which was established in the early days of NACUBO (consulting work was being done in 1967; the earliest date recorded for a meeting of the Steering Committee is December 4, 1969). The Steering Committee, under the chairmanship of Burnett A. Little, worked with Peat, Marwick, Mitchell & Co., as well as with other committees and associations, to produce a series of manuals dealing with various institutional functions and designed to assist traditionally black colleges in business and financial areas. These areas included student aid, admissions, physical plant, recordkeeping, reporting, and others.

The projects undertaken by the Steering Committee were financed first by support from the Ford Foundation and later by a grant from the Esso (now Exxon) Education Foundation. Manuals produced under the auspices of this committee and published by NACUBO helped to lay the foundations of the National Association's present publications program. Some of the early titles were revised several times over the following 10 to 15 years, and certain original manuals led to "spin-offs." The most current editions of such books form an integral part of NACUBO's inventory. An example of this process of revision and "spin-off" is given below:

Original Publication
A College Operating Manual: Planning, Budgeting, & Accounting;
    Personnel Administration; Construction Management (1969-70)

Revisions
A College Planning Cycle: People, Resources, Process—A Practical Guide
    (1975)

Management Reports (1976)

A Planning Manual for Colleges (1980)

A Management Reporting Manual for Colleges (1980)

Related Books
Wage and Salary Administration for Smaller Institutions of Higher
    Education: A Basic Guide to Management Practices (1974)

Personnel Practices for Small Colleges (1980)

In the NACUBO committee records, the last reference to the "Steering Committee on Improvements in Business Management at Predominantly Negro Colleges" is found in a copy, dated February 1971, of committee minutes for a December 1970 meeting. By July 1971, the committee's title had been shortened to "Steering Committee for Improvement of Management at Black Colleges." In July 1972 the name became simply "Management at Black Colleges Committee" or "Committee on Black Colleges" (frequently shortened to "Black Colleges Committee" in informal use), which it remained until September 1976, when the committee meeting was recorded under its final name, the "Minority Institutions Committee." In a February meeting of that year, the recommendation was made to adopt the name "Minority Institutions Committee" to reflect the broadening concerns of the group, and it was suggested that the committee be composed of blacks, native Americans, and Spanish-surnamed Americans. Although it was not always possible to have this composition, the committee was nevertheless strongly representative of minority institutions in NACUBO.

By 1972 the Committee on Black Colleges was a fully fledged standing committee of NACUBO. Primary concerns for that year included planned program budgeting, personnel, and the physical plant manual and workshop. Also in committee plans was work toward a management accounting seminar, as well as increased coordination with NACUBO's Programs for Small Colleges Committee.

At that time the Black Colleges Committee was working with the Robert R. Moton Memorial Institute, Inc., on management improvement in traditionally black institutions. The Institute is a nonprofit educational service corporation that was founded in 1952 and chartered originally in 1958 as the Robert R. Moton Memorial Foundation and Conference Center.

The Institute is named for the second president of Tuskegee Institute and successor to Booker T. Washington. Robert Moton retired in 1935 to an estate at Capahosic, Virginia, on the York River, where he held a series of informal meetings in his home that focused on subjects such as education, employment, housing, and race relations. The meetings came to be called the "Capahosic Conferences," and from them grew the Foundation and the services of the Moton Conference Center. The Moton Foundation became the Institute in 1972 when it expanded its role as a program-operating service institution. The Institute provides comprehensive services to colleges and universities, federal agencies, and various businesses and organizations in areas such as management improvement, planning, development, endowment building, and fiscal affairs.

In 1973 both the management seminar and the physical plant workshop were held (for the latter, the Committee on Black Colleges worked in cooperation with the Association of Physical Plant Administrators of Universities and Colleges, or APPA). At that time the committee was working with Texas Southern University (TSU) on that institution's MBA-CBO program (see p. 90). The Black Colleges Committee was interested in revitalizing this program in order to encourage more graduates in business management to enter college and university administration.

In connection with the Texas Southern program, the Black Colleges Committee cooperated with the Technical Assistance Consortium to Improve College Services (TACTICS). The latter was a consortium of agencies that provided technical assistance to colleges under Title III funding; members included the Moton Institute, the Central Board for College Development, and the Phelps-Stokes Foundation, among others.

The committee took part in the NACUBO Annual Meeting of 1974, presenting a session as part of the program. Also, the Black Colleges Committee presented the NACUBO board with a formal list of goals, which included identification of member institutions, identification of the pressing needs of black colleges, work toward NACUBO membership for nonmember predominantly black colleges, notifying of black colleges of literature available on college and university business, encouragement of black college participation in workshops and meetings, and possible special regional workshops designed to meet member needs. A questionnaire was sent out in an effort to plan future endeavors around black college priorities, and a recruitment letter to nonmembers was also sent. During 1974 committee membership increased from four to six.

Over the next few years, the management needs of minority institutions continued to be a primary concern of the committee, with its work centering on varying aspects of those needs. Two major issues were student financial aid, especially loan collections, and assessment of financial health, or the development of financial indicators. In spring 1977 the committee (then the Minority Institutions Committee) met jointly with the Programs for Small Colleges Committee and the Two-Year Colleges Committee to plan a constituent forum for that year's Annual Meeting.

In 1977 the problem of recruitment of black students by predominantly white institutions was discussed. The financial self-assessment workshop and a planned manual on this subject also occupied much committee time. The committee sponsored a career brochure for young people interested in entering higher education administration; the brochure was published in 1979.

The year 1980 saw the beginning of a project on which the Minority Institutions Committee worked with the United Negro College Fund (UNCF)—the Integrated Systems Approach to Institutional Management (ISATIM). This project was planned especially for colleges that were members of UNCF, of which there were 41 at the time, but it was expected that information gained during implementation of the project would carry over to benefit other small colleges that were not members.

The Minority Institutions Committee was involved with ISATIM for several years. A staff person, Mae Nash, was hired for the project, which involved site visits, training of persons to act as assessor-monitors, the development of a manual on integrated management systems, evaluation of participating institutions, and technical assistance.

Cash management, especially workshops in this area, became a major concern of the committee in 1981 and 1982. After detailed planning, three workshops on cash management were held in 1982. In fall 1983 a revised, advanced cash management workshop took place. In April 1984 the committee recommended the merger of the advanced cash management workshop with the workshops on managing investments planned for 1984-85.

One of the last projects of the committee was work with the Ford Foundation in administering a loan program for the Association of Community-

Based Education (ACBE), an organization of predominantly native American and Hispanic institutions. Work continued toward fulfillment of the goals stated in the committee's five-year plan, which was endorsed in 1983, until July 1985, when the committee merged with the Small Colleges Committee to form the Small Colleges/Minority Institutions Committee. This merger resulted from the determination that interests of the two former committees were overlapping, resulting in duplication of effort, and that NACUBO would be better served by the one new committee. However, the latter was charged to continue carrying out the special responsibilities toward minority institutions and their particular needs that had been the purview of the Minority Institutions Committee.

Chairpersons of NACUBO Minority Institutions Committee
(Formerly, Management at Black Colleges Committee)

1971-72	Burnett A. Little, Southern University, and A.L. Palmer, Howard University
1972-73	A.L. Palmer, Howard University
1973-74	Harvey R. Alexander, Johnson C. Smith University
1974-76	Caspa L. Harris, Jr., Howard University
1976-77	Curtis Holt, Jr., Benedict College
1977-79	Harold A. Jenkins, South Carolina State College
1979-81	William T. Shropshire, Huston-Tillotson College
1981-83	D.L. Brooks, Jarvis Christian College
1983-85	Robert D. Flanigan, Jr., Spelman College